520
Quick & Easy
Patchwork
Designs

520
Quick & Easy Patchwork Designs

The Amazing Paper-Folding Method for Endless Variations

Kei Kobayashi

 Sterling Publishing Co., Inc. New York

Edited by Jeanette Green
Translated from the Japanese by Sumire Fukasaku

Library of Congress Cataloging-in-Publication Data

Kobayashi, Kei.
    [Origami de tsukuru patchiwāku kiruto patān. English]
    520 quick & easy patchwork designs: the amazing paper-folding
method for endless variations / Kei Kobayashi.
       p.   cm.
    Translation of: Origami de tsukuru patchiwāku kiruto patān.
    Includes index.
    ISBN 0-8069-8508-9
    1. Patchwork—Patterns. 2. Patchwork quilts. 3. Origami.
I. Title. II. Title: 520 quick and easy patchwork designs.
III. Title: Five hundred twenty quick & easy patchwork designs.
TT835.K6313   1993
746.9'7041—dc20   92-42436
                                               CIP

2 4 6 8 10 9 7 5 3 1

Published 1993 by Sterling Publishing Company, Inc.
387 Park Avenue South, New York, N.Y. 10016
First Japanese edition published by Bunka Publishing Company
as *Patchwork Quilts Patterns (Origami de tsukuru patchiwāku
kiruto patān)* by Kei Kobayashi © 1986, 1991 by Kei Kobayashi
English translation arranged with Kei Kobayashi through the
Japan Foreign-Rights Centre © 1993 by Kei Kobayashi
Distributed in Canada by Sterling Publishing
% Canadian Manda Group, P.O. Box 920, Station U
Toronto, Ontario, Canada M8Z 5P9
Distributed in Great Britain and Europe by Cassell PLC
Villiers House, 41/47 Strand, London WC2N 5JE, England
Distributed in Australia by Capricorn Link Ltd.
P.O. Box 665, Lane Cove, NSW 2066
Manufactured in the United States of America
All rights reserved

Sterling ISBN 0-8069-8508-9

Contents

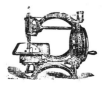

A Note from the Author

The purpose of this book is to give basic guidelines for nourishing creativity in making quilts.

The photographs of color quilts made from original origami designs (pp. 89–104) were made with the cooperation of my friends. I gave my friends ideas for the design and some advice, but the cloth and the colors were their choice. I was thrilled to see the results of their creativity, since each quilt showed the personal characteristics of the quilter's own origami design. Moreover, unforgettable bonds were developed between those of us who worked together more than three months to complete these quilts.

Creativity and individual personality, I think, are the source of originality, and these are the most important elements in quilt making. In this book, I show how to exercise your own creativity in making original quilt designs.

By making origami designs, you will not only be able to create your own original designs, but you will train your visual sense, and will find great pleasure in the discovery of the endless possibilities for your own creations as you continue to experiment with changing sizes, colors, and mixing patterns.

I hope that you will not limit yourself to the designs in this book but that you will go on to develop your own ideas, your own new quilt designs.

I want to give my heartfelt thanks to all those who helped me by making quilts. I also want to express my deep appreciation to Charles Nurnberg, vice president, and John Woodside, editorial director, both of Sterling Publishing Company, with a special note of thanks to Jeanette Green, my editor, for her unfailing patience and cooperation.

Kei Kobayashi

See chapter 4 for more design possibilities. The finished quilt is on p. 129.

1

Paper-Folding and Patchwork Design

Pieced quilts are made of juxtaposed small square and triangular pieces of cloth arranged in straight lines to form a large block. And several of these cloth blocks are arranged to create a finished quilt.

When I realized that there is a relationship between making quilts from scraps of square cloth and folding and coloring square origami paper, I became absorbed in the seemingly limitless possibilities this method offers for designing quilts. To test the utility of designing quilts with folded paper, I re-created some traditional American quilt designs. I also created original patterns by folding paper.

Patchwork is made of squares. In origami, the traditional Japanese art of paper-folding, objects are made from a thin, strong, square piece of paper. The paper-folding technique involves making creases cleanly and clearly on origami paper, often folding it into equal or unequal lengths to make triangles and squares. The geometric shapes that result from the creases on the unfolded, flattened piece of origami paper resemble miniature patchwork blocks. Geometric

shapes, after all, are the basis of European and American patchwork.

But you don't have to know anything about origami, and you don't need to have any special paper-folding skills, to try out new designs. From a small square of paper you can fold the requisite number of grids, then add diagonal and other creases, to create designs. If you cannot find any real origami paper, thin and strong squares of wrapping paper will do, but I strongly recommend using the real thing. (A paper square $2\frac{3}{4} \times 2\frac{3}{4}$ inches or 7×7 cm works well.)

After folding the paper, you simply color in the spaces made by selected squares, triangles, and other shapes to fashion your representative patchwork block in miniature. Use the unfolded back side of a piece of creased origami paper for drawing or coloring your design.

Paper-folding can be a very creative tool. This new use of origami and novel approach to design is both practical and fruitful, as you'll discover in these pages and when you start folding paper on your own.

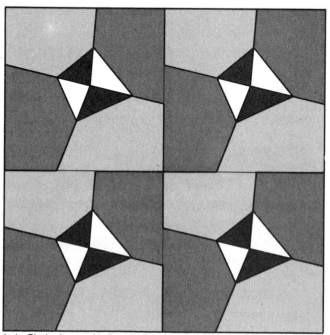

Newly Designed Block

↓ Folds

1–1   Blocks Arranged in Four-Grid

Discovering New Designs

On the American frontier, where quilting thrived from the 17th to early 19th century, paper was a precious commodity, hard to obtain. What paper people could obtain, from the broadsheets or newspapers of the East, they often oiled and used for windows in log cabins. School children wrote on slates, not paper. So, paper was not used to design quilts nor was it used to create paper quilt patterns.

In Europe, paper was occasionally used to back fabrics, such as small triangles or hexagons cut on the bias, to keep them steady. A few modern quilters also use paper for backing that eventually disintegrates in the wash, and some claim they like the crinkle of the paper. But paper patterns were not commonly used in America or Europe until the late 19th century. During the Depression of the 1930s, the *Kansas City Star* newspaper published patterns in its pages.

Today, both American and European quilt makers often draw designs for quilts on grid paper, coloring them in. Others design quilts by moving around plastic-template squares, triangles, and circles (coffee tin can lids can be cut into the desired shapes). Still others design by computer, and some even manipulate pieces of cloth.

Quilting, in early America, was a thrift craft. Most quilts were pieced from fabric scraps on hand and used to keep people warm. Since large looms could not be set up because many quilts were made while settlers travelled west in covered wagons, quilters pieced fabric into large, usually square, blocks. These blocks would not distort the shape of the finished rect-

10

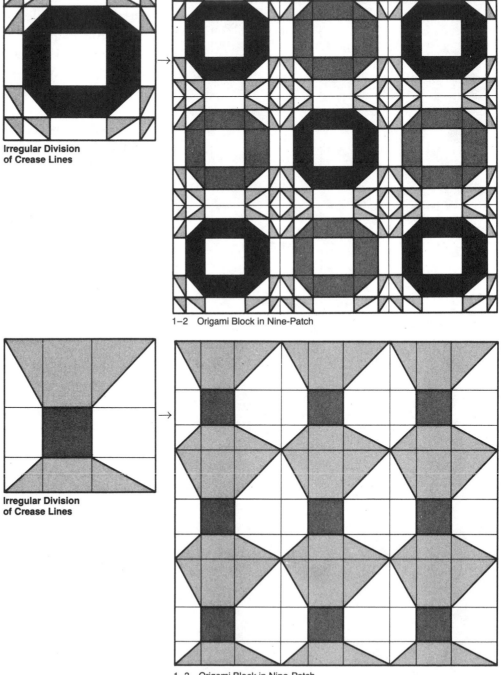

**Irregular Division
of Crease Lines**

1–2 Origami Block in Nine-Patch

**Irregular Division
of Crease Lines**

1–3 Origami Block in Nine-Patch

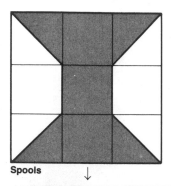

Spools   ↓

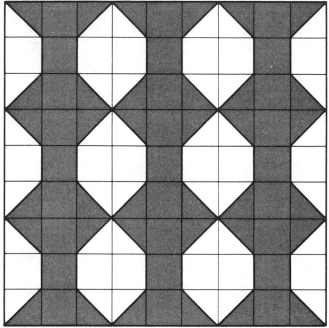

1–4   Spools (variation 1)

1–5   Spools (variation 2)

angular or square quilt. Also, the craft was very portable and could be taken to a neighbor's house, for instance, to work on while visiting.

Many quilt designs have a long tradition. The checkerboard quilt popular among American pioneers dates at least to the Middle Ages; it is mentioned in a 12th century French poem. The individual four-block pattern of the checkered quilt, like the nine-block pattern of the Irish Chain, could be repeated. Such simple motifs could easily be sewn in transit.

Over a thousand traditional American block designs have been catalogued, but the repertoire is necessarily limited because there are only a limited number of geometric forms. And because geometric forms are used as a source, many quilt designs are naturally derivative. Yet each quilt appears unique because of the quilter's choice of fabric and color, even when the design itself seems merely copied from a traditional design.

The paper-folding method for quilt design introduced in this book expands the repertoire of quilts, offering countless speedy, new design opportunities.

The use of origami is certainly not limited to the creation of traditional patterns. Even if the papers are folded irregularly and at random, the repetition of the same blocks will create a unity and a totally new design (1–1).

When the grid is equally divided, it is easy to cut and patch the pieces. However, it is not necessary to divide it equally. Irregularity can create its own charm and can lead to abstract designs (1–2 and 1–3).

However, when the grid is irregularly divided, place several origami papers under the

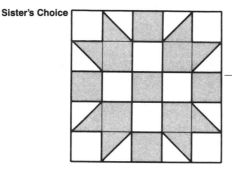
Sister's Choice

1–6 Sister's Choice and Solid Block in Chain or Checkerboard Design

original origami paper, and using an awl, pin, or other pointed object, make pinhole marks at all border and intersecting crease-line points of the design.

Let's Begin Paper-Folding

Ignore the color of the origami paper. Simply use the back side of it, to fill in the desired colors with colored markers or pencils. Then juxtapose at least nine papers so that you can see the continuous design. By changing the juxtaposition of the nine or more pieces, you'll create different relationships. And by joining the four corners of four pieces, you'll create a new design.

Or use small origami paper in several different colors on the back of a very large piece of origami paper. And arrange the colors and designs of basic blocks to your liking. By changing the colors of the linked design, you'll see yet another design (1–4 and 1–5). If you want to combine a designed block with a plain block, just place the colored origami pieces between the designed blocks. You may discover a surprising color combination (1–6).

If you combine different design blocks in the same grid, you'll achieve a fresh effect by continuing the grid division lines (1–7).

Arranging these paper blocks is much quicker than drawing variations on graph paper, and you'll be able to see the design changes instantly. It's difficult to draw a new design without having some idea in mind. However, with the origami quilt design method, you not only minimize the time it takes to develop a new design, but you can see the many unpredictable

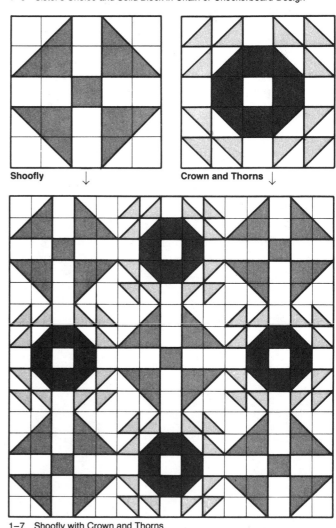
Shoofly

Crown and Thorns

1–7 Shoofly with Crown and Thorns

13

variations in the process. This will stimulate your imagination, and you may become so absorbed, as I was on discovering this new tool, that you even forget to sleep.

When you juxtapose the finished blocks, you will see a surprising new continuous design. The results are often beautiful and the possibilities endless. For a few folds, you'll be richly rewarded and eager to create your one-of-a-kind quilt.

Discovering Sources for Original Designs

The fun of making quilts comes not simply from sewing individual blocks, but from deciding where to place the blocks next to each other. This is one of the most creative parts of quilt making.

When you use origami to create blocks, you can plan ahead. This process nourishes both the analytical mind and the creative spirit, while broadening your perspective. When you begin to see the world in terms of visual images, you realize that everything around you can become a source for your own designs. With practice, your sense of design will develop naturally.

When you're at a loss thinking about designs, find some origami paper and fold it casually in any way you like.

Once you understand the structure of block designing with origami, you'll easily make traditional block designs. As you try them out with origami paper, you'll be able to anticipate what the finished structure will look like when the blocks are finally pieced together.

Folding origami paper also offers good training for your eye, since this activity helps you learn to see the underlying structural design in the many things around you—buildings, pavements, carpets, windows, floors. It will help you find motifs in places that you were once unaware of.

Simple origami folds can be the source of limitless graphic designs. Since *you* are the designer, you can freely take advantage of the infinite possibilities for your own creations.

2

An Innovative Approach to Quilt Design

Dispense with Graph Paper

Is it easy to begin making a quilt whenever you want? Since there are pictures of so many wonderful quilts, you can hardly make up your mind. And since quilt making is so time-consuming, you'd probably rather make a quilt that you designed and that pleases you. But how? With colored pencils or marker and graph paper on your desk, you wonder where to begin. Some of you may have discovered many things by coloring already. But with graph paper you must draw in the whole page to see the different patterns your blocks create.

However, with origami paper you can make several quilt blocks by just changing the arrangement of the papers. You can see as many possibilities as though you were looking through a kaleidoscope. Change the color, replace this and that piece, place them next to various patterns, or just change directions. In short, move the folded paper around as you

please, and you will find a seemingly endless number of interesting designs.

However, keep in mind that these origami blocks only prepare you to make the actual designs. You don't need to fold them neatly or color them meticulously. Anybody can do this. So, together with your family and friends, even with small children, you can multiply your ideas. And quilt design, like quilt making, can assume its traditional place as a community art.

If your family and friends become participants in the design process, they will all be very interested in the outcome. This will encourage you to continue your work, and the final product is bound to become a family treasure.

Paper-Folding Advantages

Origami designs have many advantages. Paper folding nourishes your design sense, improves originality, helps you easily arrange blocks and make your own pattern and template. Graph

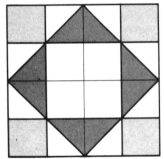

King's Crown

2–1   King's Crown

paper drafting is unnecessary, and you can even embellish with appliqué.

Pattern Drafting Is Unnecessary

For those unfamiliar with graph paper, using it for drafting must be very bothersome. With origami, you avoid the troublesome work of using rulers and counting small squares. Just fold the paper, making the necessary grid or crease line for the design you have in mind, and color in the spaces. That's all there is to drafting patterns, whether for traditional, variations on traditional, or your own original designs.

Origami Nourishes Your Design Sense

In order to fold origami paper for the necessary creases, you must be able to visualize the structure of geometric designs. Once you get a sense of how to discern a pattern by observation, you will develop a new interest in looking at objects around you.

Origami Improves Your Originality

Origami will not only help you re-create traditional patterns, but by coloring in spaces created by irregular, freely folded creases, you'll also be able to make original contemporary designs. Even for beginners, it's easy to create original designs with this method.

Use Origami for Setting Blocks

To complete a quilt design on graph paper is time consuming. In addition, to determine all the variations that result from changing the directions of a given block, you need to start all over again on a new sheet.

Many quilt makers skip this stage, and when

16

they complete a block design, they make as many copies as necessary and arrange them on the floor. Only then can they determine the relationships between the blocks. However, with an origami miniature, you can work at your desk or on your kitchen table and arrange individual blocks in many ways to see the various design possibilities. It makes a big difference to see your design possibilities before you make blocks in cloth.

If you use a single block on graph paper, it's hard to visualize the design as a whole. By using two blocks, you may discover the possibility for quite another overall design, or a chain effect, which you would not have been able to see by looking at a single block. By arranging several origami blocks, you can see the whole at once.

If you change the color in one part, there is already another entirely new design. It would be too late to see this change if you were doing this by arranging the actual cloth blocks.

With origami block setting, you not only easily see the possible variations for a design before you begin the quilt, but you can see the new design as a whole (2–1).

Make Your Own Pattern the Size You Want

When you use ready-made patterns, you often have to adjust the size. By making your own pattern, you don't have to depend on ready-made patterns, and this will give you confidence and the ability to create. If the quilt you plan to make is rectangular, divide the shorter length of the rectangle into equal parts. The length of one part will serve as a template for your block.

You can also make an appliqué design from a found image, such as that on an art postcard. Simply enlarge or reduce the image until it is the size you want to use for appliqué. Here's how.

Enlarge two copies of the postcard or other image until the image becomes 11 × 17 inches (27.5 × 42.5 cm), the biggest standard paper size for most photocopy machines. Fold one of the photocopies (11 × 17 inches) into fourths widthwise and into sixths lengthwise, which will create 24 square blocks. Number each block 1 through 24. Keep this sheet as a record. Fold the second photocopy just like the first, and cut out the 24 blocks. Then enlarge each individual block on a photocopy machine until it is 11 × 11 inches (27.5 × 27.5 cm). Using this method, you can make a larger or smaller image, dividing and enlarging or reducing the image to meet your specifications.

You Can Make the Template Easily As Well

It is essential that you fold your template accurately. Cut the actual size of the creased pieces carefully. Paste them on cardboard, add ¼-inch (5-mm) margins all around, and cut out the pieces. These pieces will serve as templates when you cut the fabric. Make only the necessary pattern pieces, since some will be used repeatedly in a given block. Keep the miniature blocks for your own reference.

To make an appliqué template, cut out your cardboard image outline precisely. Mark your fabric with the template, and sew the appliqué outline on your machine. *After* you sew the outline of the shape, cut out the appliqué piece from the fabric, adding ⅛-inch (2- to 3-mm) seam allowance. If you cut out the appliqué first, *before* you sew the outline, the appliqué piece is unlikely to retain its shape because fabric grain moves and can be hard to control. For professional results, place the image on the quilt with a few pins, then turn under the seam allowance and pin. Then, stitch the appliqué shape catching the machine seam outline, by hand. This will allow you to re-create the exact outline of the image. Finally, stitch your appliqué in place on your quilt.

3

Creating Block Patterns with Origami

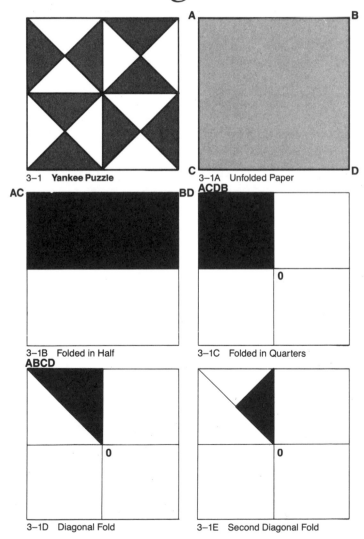

3–1 **Yankee Puzzle**

3–1A Unfolded Paper

3–1B Folded in Half

3–1C Folded in Quarters

3–1D Diagonal Fold

3–1E Second Diagonal Fold

The ideal size for origami paper is rather small (3 inches square). If you cannot get that size, cut a 6-inch square origami paper into four pieces. If the origami paper is too big, it takes a lot of time to color, and a larger space will be required for juxtaposing blocks. With smaller origami paper you can work faster in a small space, and you will readily be able to see the overall design. The color of the origami paper doesn't matter, since your coloring will be done on the back side.

Throughout this book, the *dark* shaded sections of the illustrations represent the colored side of origami paper, and the *light* shaded sections represent the uncolored, backside of origami paper. The lines on the white blocks indicate folding guidelines.

Those blocks with captioned pattern names and illustration numbers (such as 3–1) represent designs made by the folding lines when the block is opened up and color is added.

Basic Rules for Paper-Folding

1. Place the origami paper on a table, with the colored side down (3–1A).
2. Keep the positions of corners A, B, C, and D so that any diagonal lines will run in the same direction (3–1A).

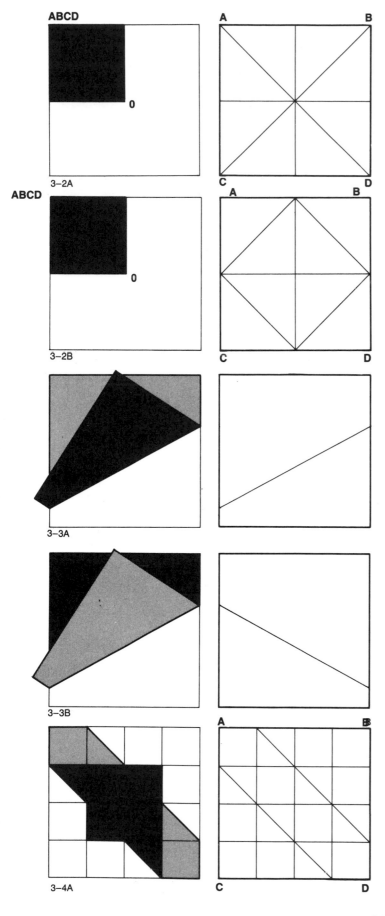

3–2A

3–2B

3–3A

3–3B

3–4A

3. First fold the basic grid lines (3–1B and 3–1C). Then open the fold before folding again for the pattern lines (3–1D and 3–1E).

4. Open the folds again and color the spaces made by the creases with magic markers. This is your design. Our example, Yankee Puzzle (3–1), was created from the series of folds shown. The paper was then unfolded, laid flat, and selected triangles colored in.

5. Keep the colored blocks, since they will be helpful for trying to see the many design variations.

Now let's begin to fold, following the example, the Yankee Puzzle block pattern (see 3–1).

Mark A B C D in each corner (3–1A) of the origami paper. Keep the colored side down and fold with the plain back side up. Fold the origami paper in half (3–1B) and in half again (3–1C) to make four squares (a four-patch grid). Crease diagonal lines from ACDB to the central point (3–1D). Then fold the triangles you've just made into two again (3–1E). Open the origami paper, and color in the spaces (3–1, Yankee Puzzle).

When you fold the paper, you may move the origami shape freely, but the illustration showing the process of folding will always be placed in the same ABCD position. Keep this orientation in mind to save confusion.

In some cases, you may have to turn the origami paper around as you fold, but the steps for folding will remain the same as in the illustrations. As shown in 3–2A and 3–2B, folding can be done two ways—from the center to the corner (top left corner of 3–2A) or from the midpoints of the two sides (see diagonal line of 3–2B). Please note that the direction of the diagonal lines will necessarily be different depending on which way you fold. See the results from the illustrations beside the folding examples shown here.

Also, don't mix the front and the back sides of the origami when folding irregular diagonal lines (see examples 3–3A and 3–3B and their results).

To make diagonal folds symmetrically (3–4), make the creases after opening the basic four-

Grid and Patch Creases

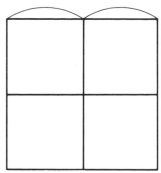

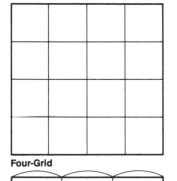

3–5 **Four-Patch**

Four-Grid   Eight-Grid

grid fold. The arrows on the illustrations indicate results of given folds. See how 3–4A creates the creases for 3–4. The creases must always be firm and clear.

Basic Grid Divisions

When a block pattern is made of four squares, with each side divided into two, it is called a *Four-Patch* pattern. This can be varied to *four grids* when the sides are divided into four, and to *eight grids* with eight divisions (3–5).

When the paper or cloth square or block is divided equally into three, making nine squares, it is called a *Nine-Patch* pattern with *three grids*. Variations of this pattern are made with *six grids* and *nine grids* (3–6). The square block can also be divided into *five grids* and *seven grids* (3–7).

Most block patterns are made with symmetrical triangles, and many patterns divided by even numbers are made by repeating one-fourth of the pattern. Make diagonal lines after folding the grid first and opening the paper. Then fold the paper diagonally as shown in 3–8. For 3–8A, the origami paper is kept in quarters (folded in half, then in half, again) and finally folded at the top left corner and the lower right corner into diagonals, thus creating the pattern outlined.

Here's how to discern grid divisions.

Find the Smallest Piece

From the smallest piece, find the number of equal divisions in order to see how many grids or squares there are. The pattern in 3–9 has a small isosceles triangle that's one-eighth the

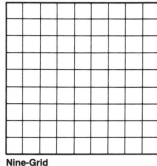

3–6 **Three-Grid (Nine-Patch)**

Six-Grid   Nine-Grid

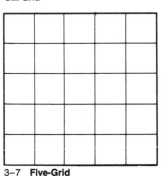

3–7 *Five-Grid*   Seven-Grid

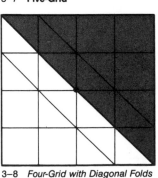

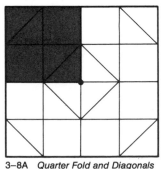

3–8 *Four-Grid with Diagonal Folds*   3–8A *Quarter Fold and Diagonals*

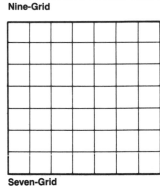

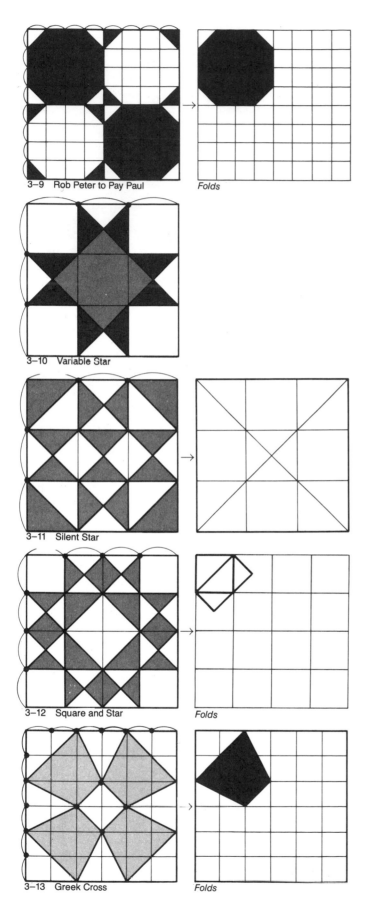

3-9 Rob Peter to Pay Paul

Folds

3-10 Variable Star

3-11 Silent Star

3-12 Square and Star

Folds

3-13 Greek Cross

Folds

side of the square. Therefore, there are eight grids. If you see that four similar patterns are placed symmetrically in a block, you can tell that they were made by opening four folds.

Find Grid Divisions by the Diagonal Lines

Examine the pattern carefully in order to identify the structure of the block, and then find the number of grids by finding the starting point of the diagonal lines.

For example, the pattern Variable Star (3–10) has three grids because there are three divisions on each side (which creates a nine-patch block; $3 \times 3 = 9$). Therefore, you can start making diagonal lines from these division points.

When the diagonal line is in the center, fold the grid and the diagonal of the grid first; then open the fold to make the crease for the central diagonal line, as shown in the block Silent Star (3–11).

The pattern in the Square and Star block (3–12) is for four grids, which is a repetition of the one-quarter fold. When you open this, the pattern is already completed.

However, as shown in Greek Cross (3–13), a side may be divided into three grids, but you must fold it into six grids to get the division point for the central square. This pattern is also a one-quarter repetition, which means you can use four folds.

Find the Number of Grids by Diagonal Lines and Color Divisions

The Variable Star pattern (3–14) is divided into three, but you can use the one-quarter repetition or you can fold it into six grids.

For Short, Fine Lines, Draw in Extended Creases

When some parts of the grids have diagonal lines, it is sometimes simpler to extend them by drawing them in rather than by folding the creases (see 3–15 and 3–16).

The Nine-Patch pattern (3–17) can be easily made by folding the three grids first, and then dividing the central part into three equal grids by drawing in the lines.

Also, when the pattern is partly appliquéd, it is useful to draw those parts in by hand—see the Flower Basket (3–18) and the Maple Leaf (3–19).

Make Circles by Grid Division

Patterns of circles and arcs can be easily made with a compass, using the side of the grid as a radius—see the Melon Patch (3–20) and the Mill Wheel (3–21).

At this stage, origami block patterns may be used for seeing the possibilities for divisions and for the continuation of the designs. Since you are not yet cutting the actual cloth, these division lines do not have to be accurate. Unless divisions are so minute, you can fold three origami papers simultaneously. Just be careful to make the creases sharp and clear.

Let's fold origami paper now, based on grid divisions. In the pages that follow (pp. 24–32 and 49–81), see examples of four-patch, three-patch, three-grid, four-grid, five-grid, six-grid, seven-grid, eight-grid, nine-grid, and other patterns.

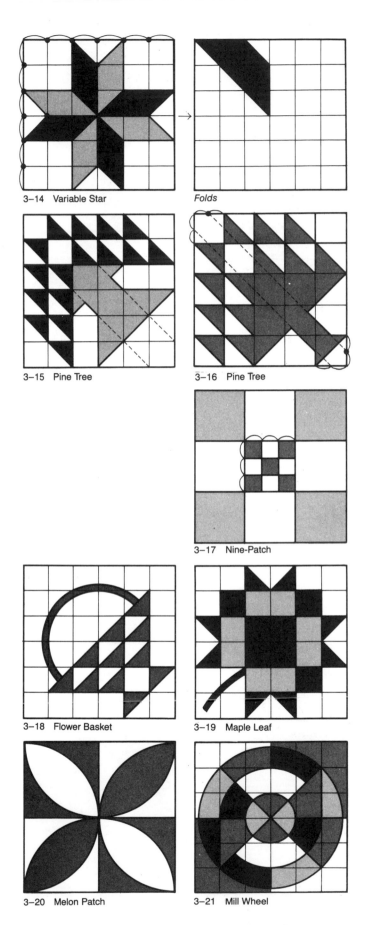

3–14 Variable Star

Folds

3–15 Pine Tree

3–16 Pine Tree

3–17 Nine-Patch

3–18 Flower Basket

3–19 Maple Leaf

3–20 Melon Patch

3–21 Mill Wheel

23

Four-Patch

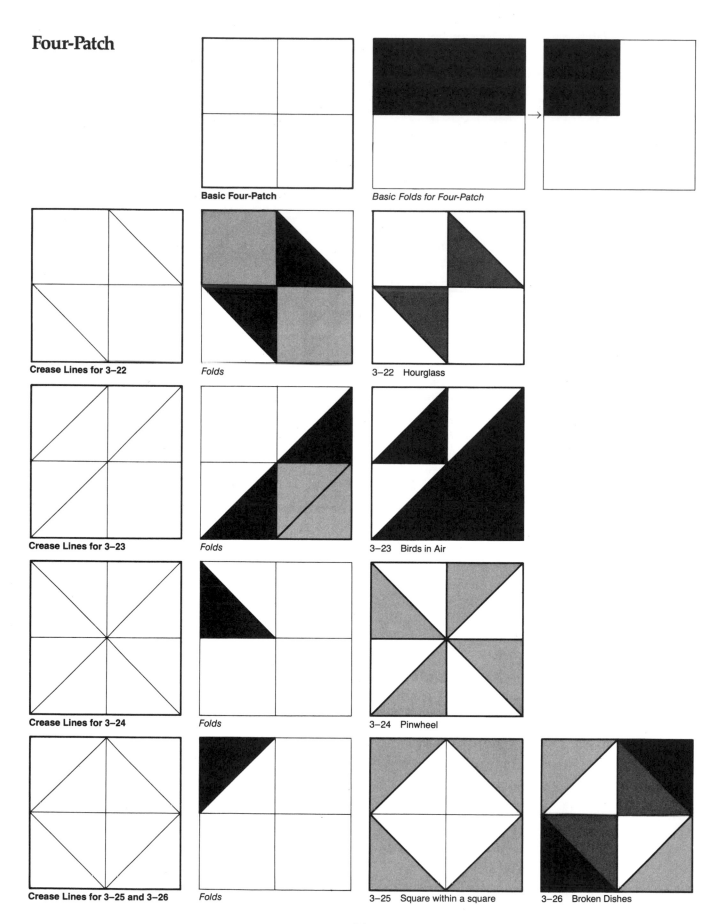

Basic Four-Patch

Basic Folds for Four-Patch

Crease Lines for 3–22

Folds

3–22   Hourglass

Crease Lines for 3–23

Folds

3–23   Birds in Air

Crease Lines for 3–24

Folds

3–24   Pinwheel

Crease Lines for 3–25 and 3–26

Folds

3–25   Square within a square

3–26   Broken Dishes

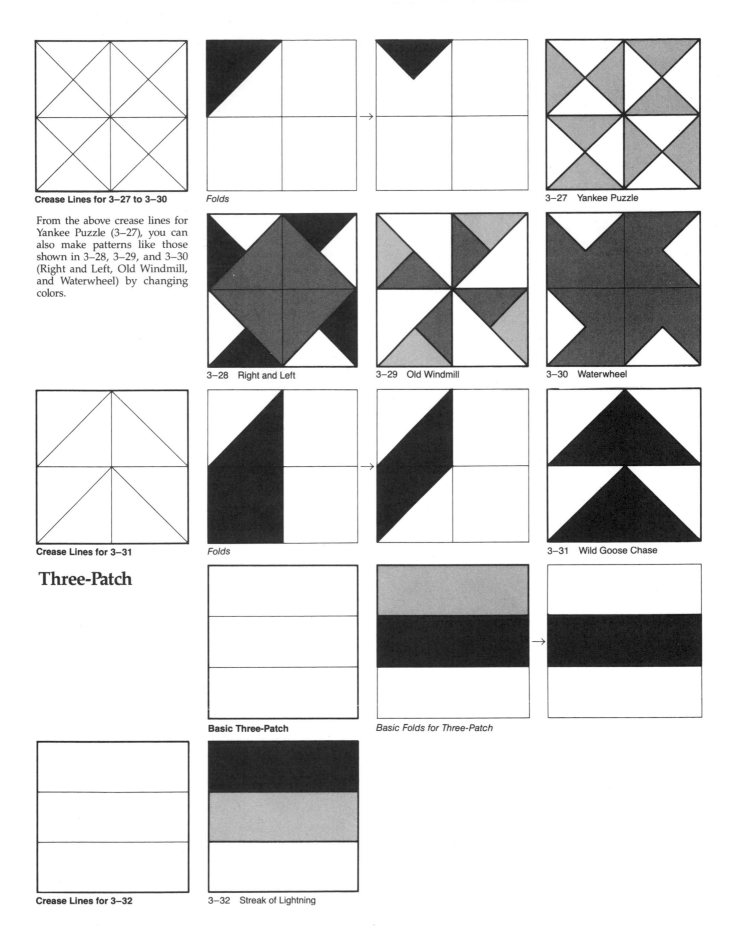

Crease Lines for 3–27 to 3–30

Folds

3–27 Yankee Puzzle

From the above crease lines for Yankee Puzzle (3–27), you can also make patterns like those shown in 3–28, 3–29, and 3–30 (Right and Left, Old Windmill, and Waterwheel) by changing colors.

3–28 Right and Left

3–29 Old Windmill

3–30 Waterwheel

Crease Lines for 3–31

Folds

3–31 Wild Goose Chase

Three-Patch

Basic Three-Patch

Basic Folds for Three-Patch

Crease Lines for 3–32

3–32 Streak of Lightning

25

Three-Grid

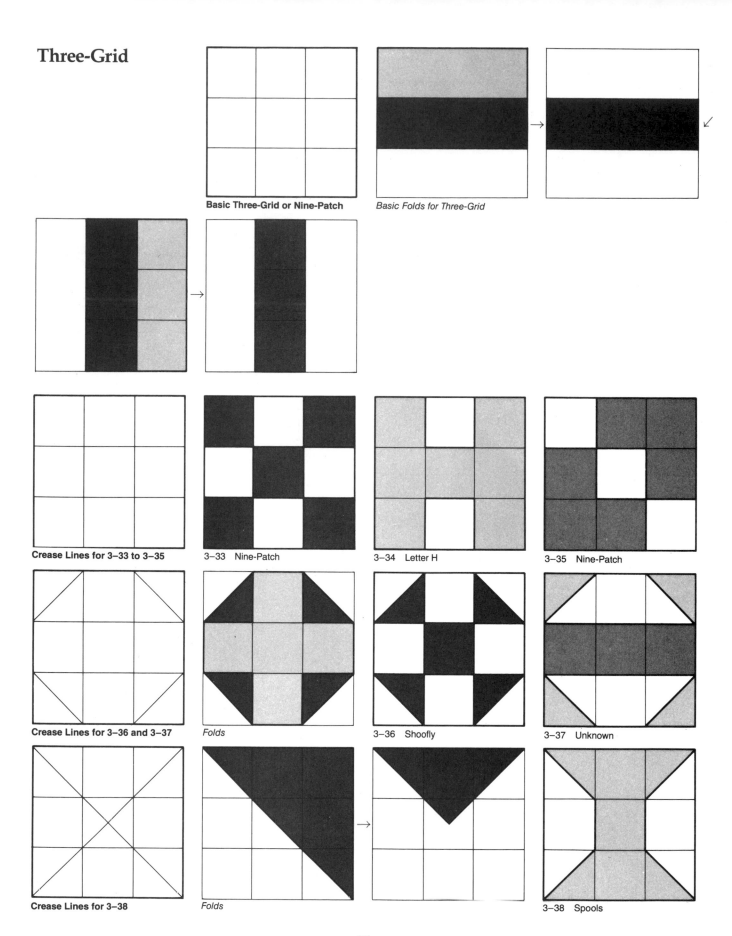

Basic Three-Grid or Nine-Patch

Basic Folds for Three-Grid

Crease Lines for 3–33 to 3–35

3–33 Nine-Patch

3–34 Letter H

3–35 Nine-Patch

Crease Lines for 3–36 and 3–37

Folds

3–36 Shoofly

3–37 Unknown

Crease Lines for 3–38

Folds

3–38 Spools

26

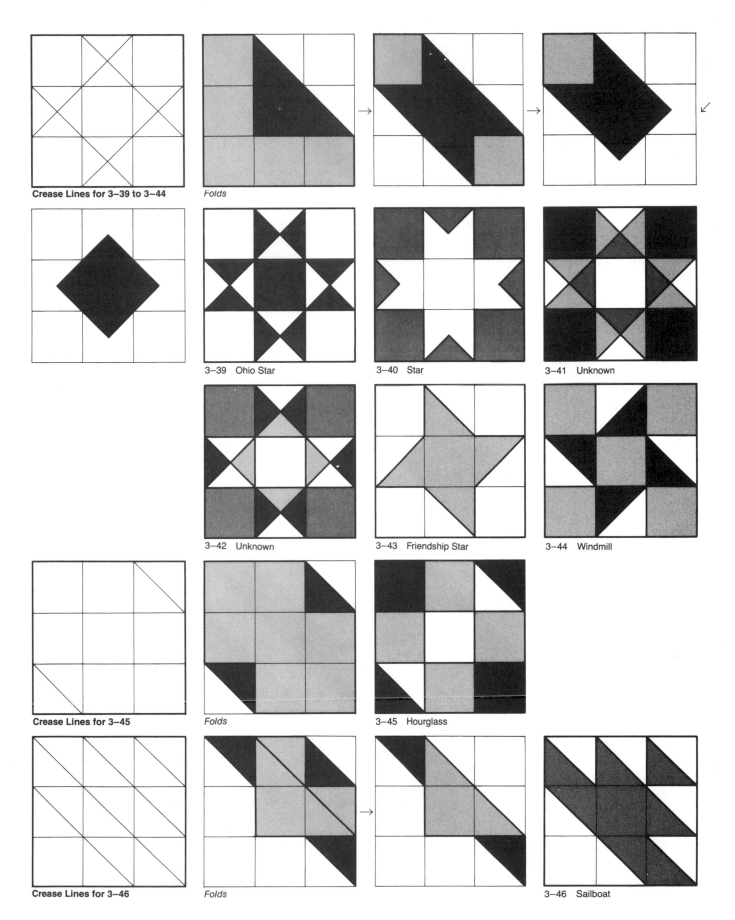

Crease Lines for 3–39 to 3–44

Folds

3–39 Ohio Star

3–40 Star

3–41 Unknown

3–42 Unknown

3–43 Friendship Star

3–44 Windmill

Crease Lines for 3–45

Folds

3–45 Hourglass

Crease Lines for 3–46

Folds

3–46 Sailboat

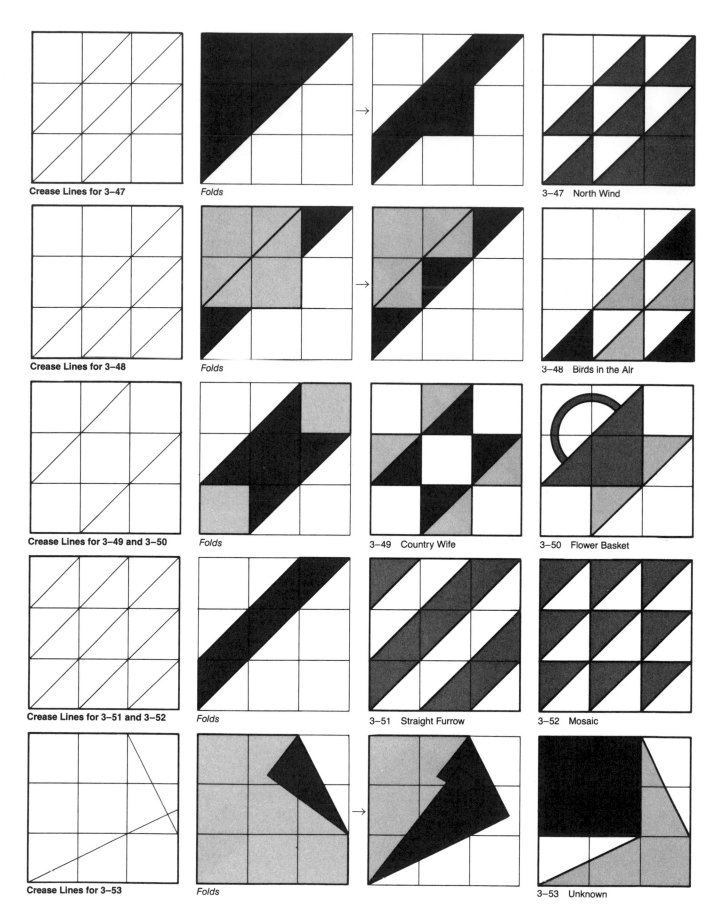

Crease Lines for 3–47

Folds

3–47 North Wind

Crease Lines for 3–48

Folds

3–48 Birds in the Air

Crease Lines for 3–49 and 3–50

Folds

3–49 Country Wife

3–50 Flower Basket

Crease Lines for 3–51 and 3–52

Folds

3–51 Straight Furrow

3–52 Mosaic

Crease Lines for 3–53

Folds

3–53 Unknown

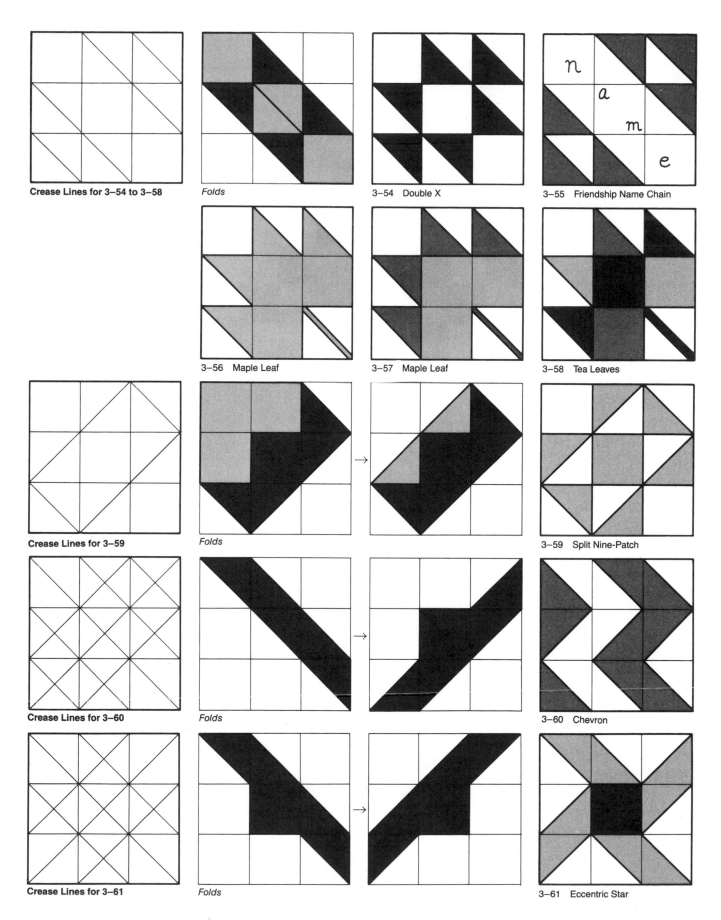

Crease Lines for 3–54 to 3–58

Folds

3–54 Double X

3–55 Friendship Name Chain

3–56 Maple Leaf

3–57 Maple Leaf

3–58 Tea Leaves

Crease Lines for 3–59

Folds

3–59 Split Nine-Patch

Crease Lines for 3–60

Folds

3–60 Chevron

Crease Lines for 3–61

Folds

3–61 Eccentric Star

Four-Grid

Basic Four-Grid

Basic Folds for Four-Grid

Open and change direction.

Crease Lines for 3–62 to 3–67

3–62   Mosaic Nine-Patch

3–63   Four-Patch

3–64   Four-Patch

3–65   Tam's Patch

3–66   Autumn Leaf

3–67   Eight-Patch Variation

Crease Lines for 3–68

Folds

3–68   Lady of the Lake

Crease Lines for 3–69 and 3–70

Folds

3–69   Jacob's Ladder

3–70   Northern Star

30

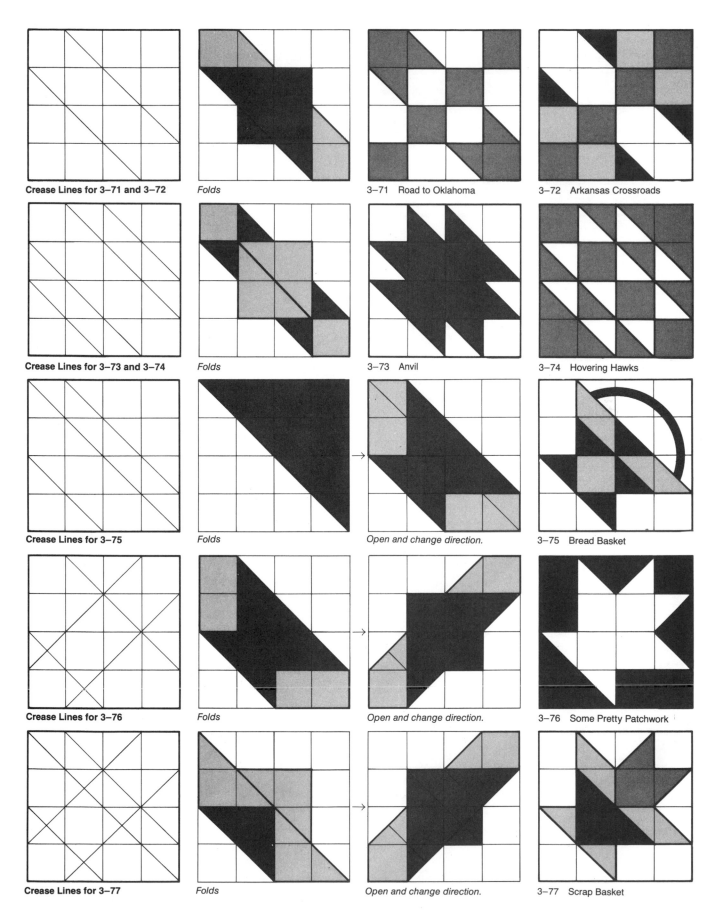

Crease Lines for 3–71 and 3–72

Folds

3–71   Road to Oklahoma

3–72   Arkansas Crossroads

Crease Lines for 3–73 and 3–74

Folds

3–73   Anvil

3–74   Hovering Hawks

Crease Lines for 3–75

Folds

Open and change direction.

3–75   Bread Basket

Crease Lines for 3–76

Folds

Open and change direction.

3–76   Some Pretty Patchwork

Crease Lines for 3–77

Folds

Open and change direction.

3–77   Scrap Basket

31

Crease Lines for 3–78   *Folds*   3–78 Sawtooth

Crease Lines for 3–79   *Folds*   3–79 Sawtooth

Crease Lines for 3–80   *Folds*   *Open and change direction.*   3–80 Indian Trail

Crease Lines for 3–81 to 3–83   *Folds*

3–81 Mosaic   3–82 Ocean Waves   3–83 Streak of Lightning

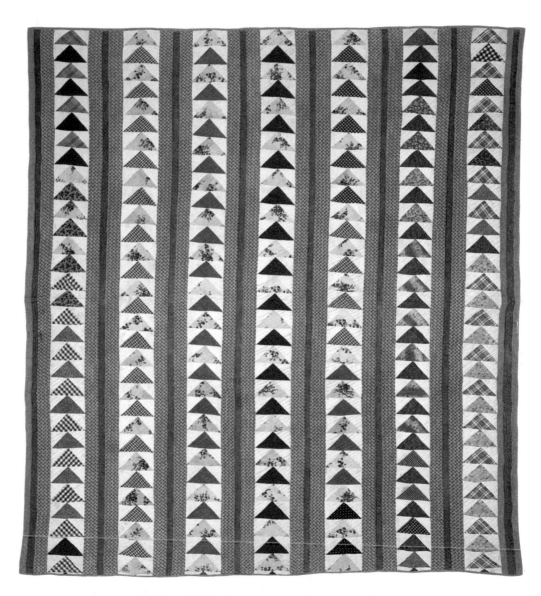

3–31 **Wild Goose Chase** Maine, 1900s
88 × 80 inches (220 × 200 cm)
cotton (four-patch)

3–32 **Streak of Lightning** Rhode Island, 1880
92 × 72 inches (230 × 180 cm)
home-spun cotton (three-patch)

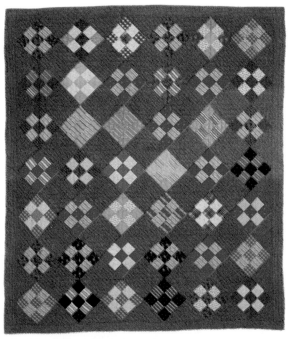

3–33 **Nine-Patch** Massachusetts, 1870
74 × 65 inches (185 × 162 cm)
cotton (three-grid)

3–36 **Shoofly** Maine, 1890
83 × 80 inches (207 × 200 cm)
cotton (three-grid)

3–39 **Ohio Star** New York, 19th century
92 × 82 inches (230 × 205 cm)
cotton (three-grid)

3–68 **Lady of the Lake** Pennsylvania, 1880
70 × 56 inches (175 × 140 cm)
cotton (four-grid)

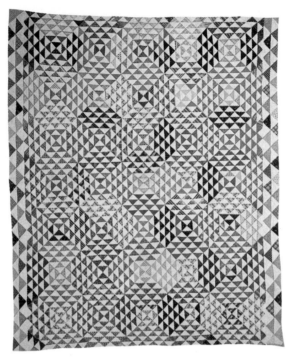

3–82 **Ocean Waves** Connecticut, 1860
86 × 72 inches (215 × 180 cm)
cotton (four-grid)

3–122 **Star** Maine, 1840
82 × 78 inches (205 × 195 cm)
cotton (four-grid)

3–154 **Monkey Wrench** New York, 1880
66 × 66 inches (165 × 165 cm)
cotton (five-grid)

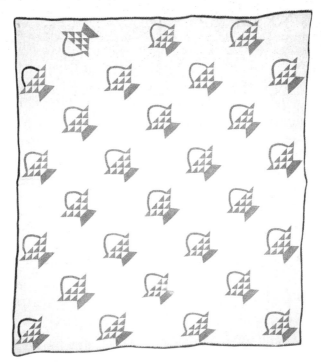

3–189 **Basket** New York, 1860
77 × 68 inches (192 × 170 cm)
cotton

38

3–201 **Double Nine-Patch** Massachusetts, 1800s
90 × 86 inches (225 × 215 cm)
cotton (six-grid)

3–252 **Pine Tree** New York, 1870
72 × 68 inches (180 × 170 cm)
cotton (six-grid)

3–265 **Birds in Air** New York, 1880
70 × 60 inches (175 × 150 cm)
cotton (seven-grid)

3–272 **Basket** Connecticut, 1870
82 × 80 inches (205 × 200 cm)
cotton

3–291 **Wild Goose Chase** New York, 1870
94 × 89 inches (235 × 222 cm)
cotton

3–350 **Steeple Chase** New York, 1880
82 × 66 inches (205 × 165 cm)
cotton

3–353 **Rising Sun** Pennsylvania, 1870
84 × 84 inches (210 × 210 cm)
cotton (eight-grid)

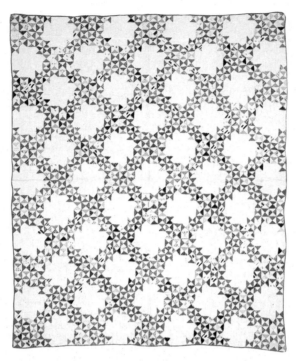

3–355 **Hourglass** New York, 1890
80 × 66 inches (200 × 165 cm)
cotton (four-grid)

3–356 **Double Irish Chain** Maine, 1870
88 × 74 inches (220 × 185 cm)
cotton (five-grid)

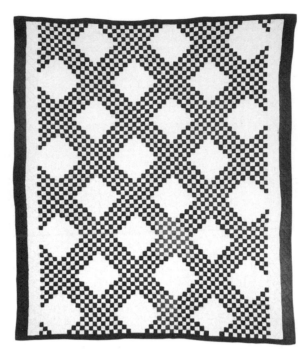

3–357 **Triple Irish Chain** Pennsylvania, 1890
80 × 70 inches (200 × 175 cm)
cotton (nine-grid)

3–358 **Hexagon Stars** Ohio, 1890
75 × 63 inches (187 × 157 cm)
cotton (hexagon)

3–359 **Lone Star**   New York, 1900
88 × 88 inches (220 × 220 cm)
cotton (octagon)

3–360 **Lone Star** Massachusetts, 1840
71 × 71 inches (177 × 177 cm)
silk (octagon)

3–361 **Star Variations** New York, 1870
98 × 98 inches (245 × 245 cm)
cotton (octagon)

3–362 **Diamond Star** New York, 1860
84 × 70 inches (210 × 175 cm)
cotton (octagon)

3–363 **Sunflower** Massachusetts, 1850
96 × 96 inches (240 × 240 cm)
cotton chintz (octagon)

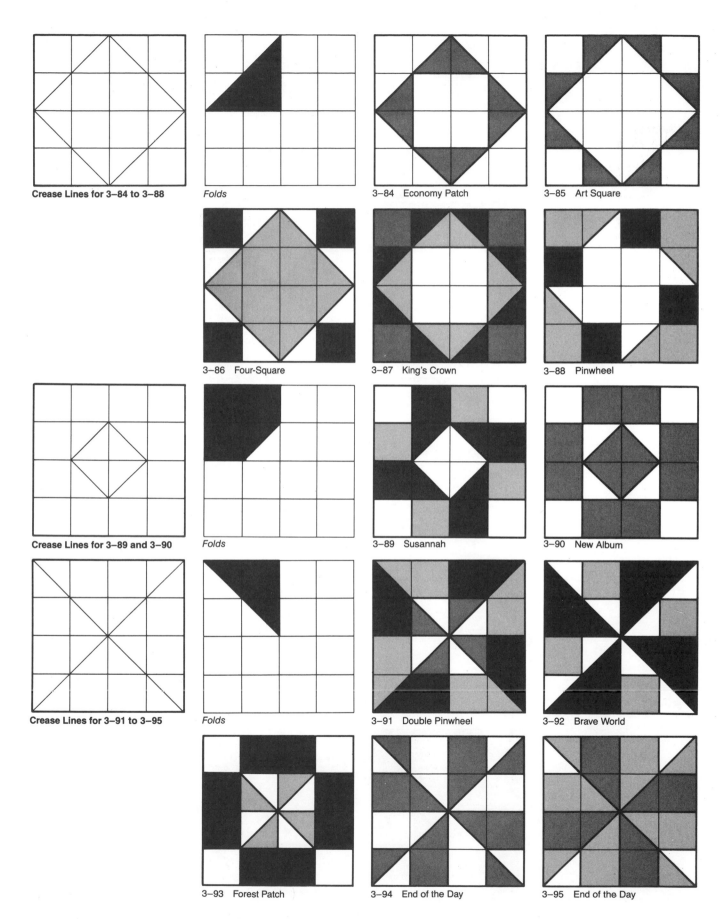

Crease Lines for 3–84 to 3–88

Folds

3–84 Economy Patch

3–85 Art Square

3–86 Four-Square

3–87 King's Crown

3–88 Pinwheel

Crease Lines for 3–89 and 3–90

Folds

3–89 Susannah

3–90 New Album

Crease Lines for 3–91 to 3–95

Folds

3–91 Double Pinwheel

3–92 Brave World

3–93 Forest Patch

3–94 End of the Day

3–95 End of the Day

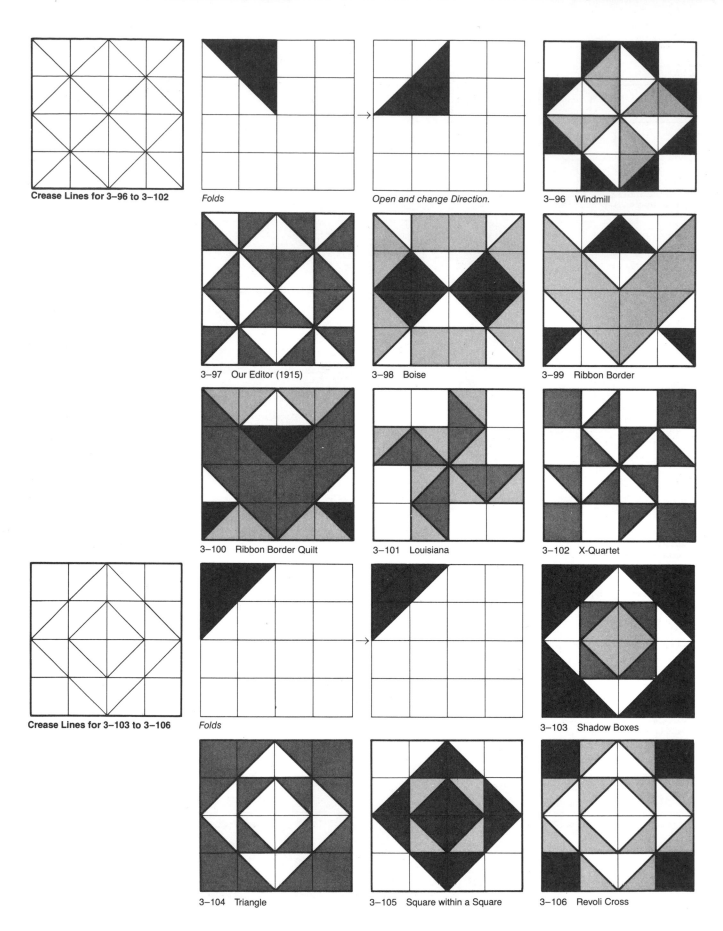

Crease Lines for 3–96 to 3–102

Folds

Open and change Direction.

3–96   Windmill

3–97   Our Editor (1915)

3–98   Boise

3–99   Ribbon Border

3–100   Ribbon Border Quilt

3–101   Louisiana

3–102   X-Quartet

Crease Lines for 3–103 to 3–106

Folds

3–103   Shadow Boxes

3–104   Triangle

3–105   Square within a Square

3–106   Revoli Cross

Crease Lines for 3–107 to 3–113

Folds

3–107   Kansas Dugout

3–108   Mosaic

3–109   Mosaic

3–110   Mosaic

3–111   Connecticut (1920–1930)

3–112   Grandpa's Favorite

3–113   Mosaic

Crease Lines for 3–114 to 3–117

Folds

Open and change direction.

3–114   Whirlpool

3–115   Balkan Puzzle

3–116   Wind-Blown Square

3–117   Blockade

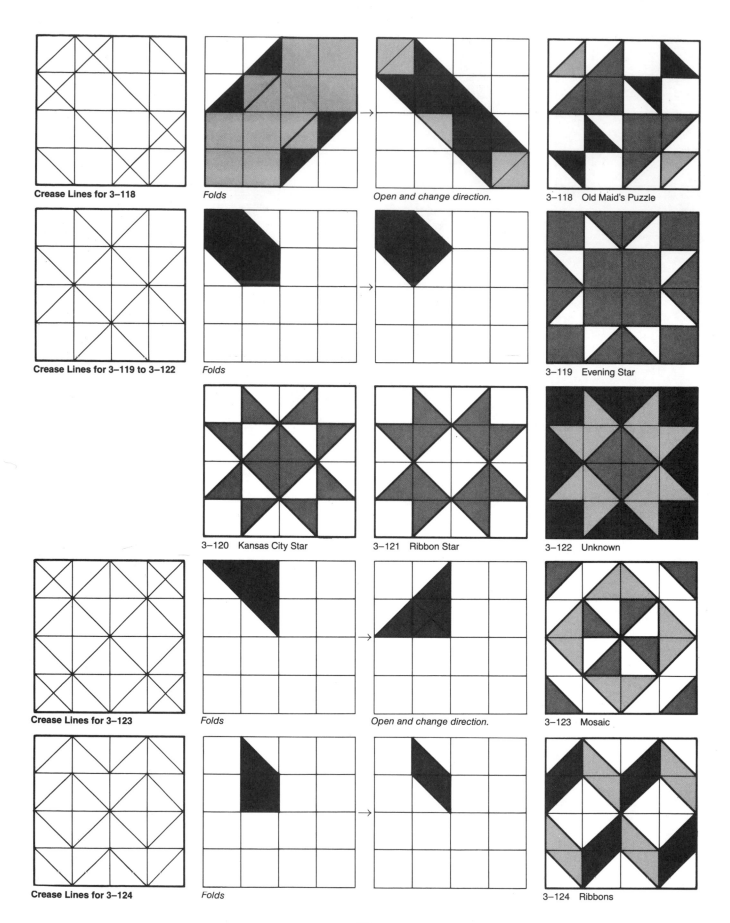

Crease Lines for 3–118

Folds

Open and change direction.

3–118   Old Maid's Puzzle

Crease Lines for 3–119 to 3–122

Folds

3–119   Evening Star

3–120   Kansas City Star

3–121   Ribbon Star

3–122   Unknown

Crease Lines for 3–123

Folds

Open and change direction.

3–123   Mosaic

Crease Lines for 3–124

Folds

3–124   Ribbons

52

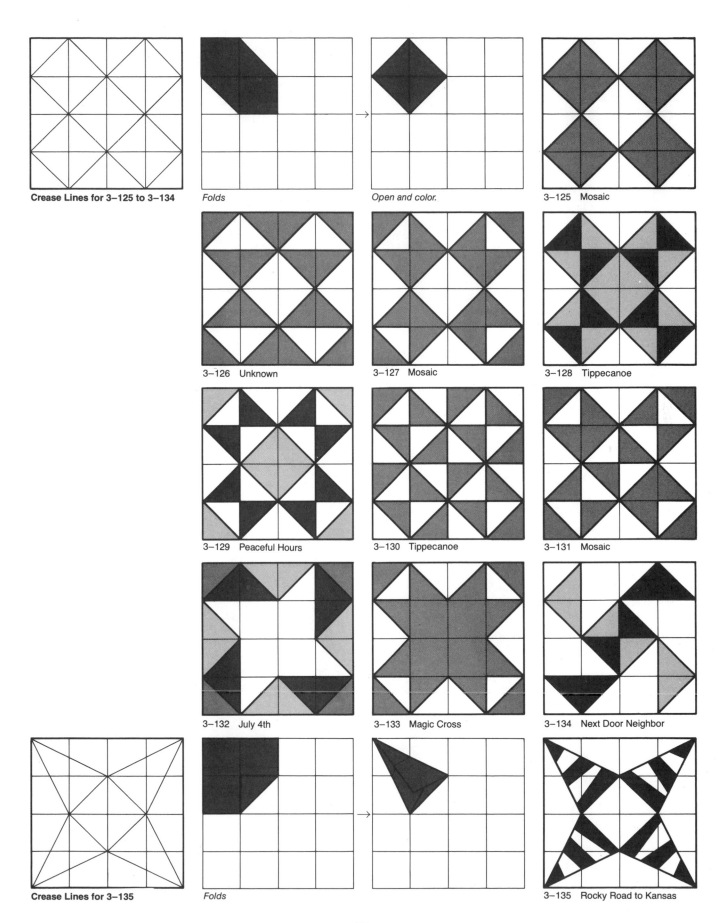

Crease Lines for 3–125 to 3–134

Folds

Open and color.

3–125 Mosaic

3–126 Unknown

3–127 Mosaic

3–128 Tippecanoe

3–129 Peaceful Hours

3–130 Tippecanoe

3–131 Mosaic

3–132 July 4th

3–133 Magic Cross

3–134 Next Door Neighbor

Crease Lines for 3–135

Folds

3–135 Rocky Road to Kansas

53

Crease Lines for 3–136

Folds

3–136   Star of the Milky Way

Crease Lines for 3–137

Folds

3–137   Six-Point Star

Crease Lines for 3–138

Folds

3–138   Widows

Crease Lines for 3–139

Folds

3–139   Unknown

Five-Grid

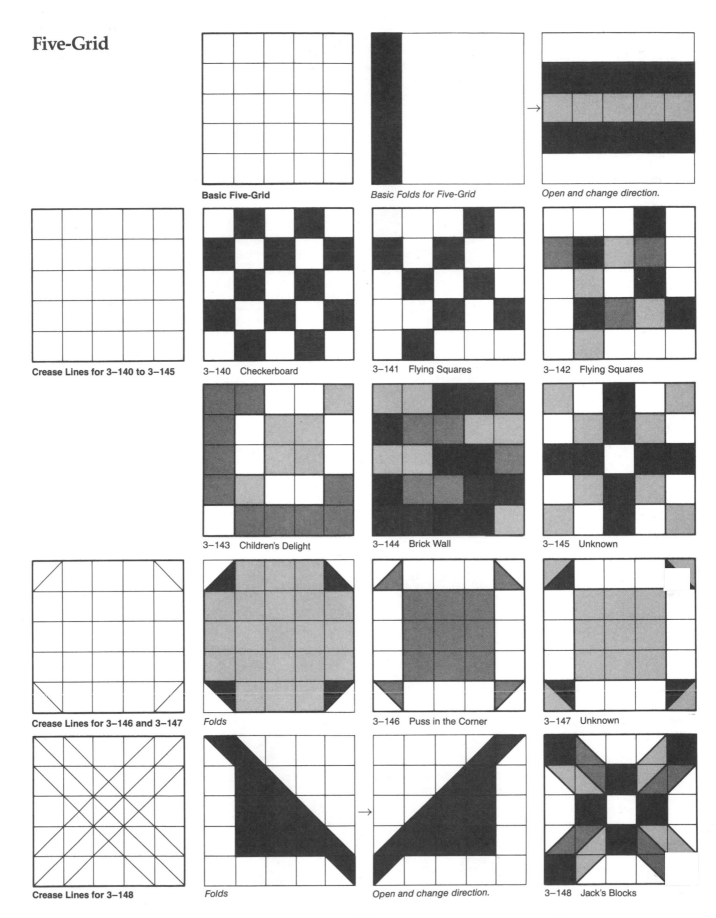

Basic Five-Grid

Basic Folds for Five-Grid

Open and change direction.

Crease Lines for 3–140 to 3–145

3–140   Checkerboard

3–141   Flying Squares

3–142   Flying Squares

3–143   Children's Delight

3–144   Brick Wall

3–145   Unknown

Crease Lines for 3–146 and 3–147

Folds

3–146   Puss in the Corner

3–147   Unknown

Crease Lines for 3–148

Folds

Open and change direction.

3–148   Jack's Blocks

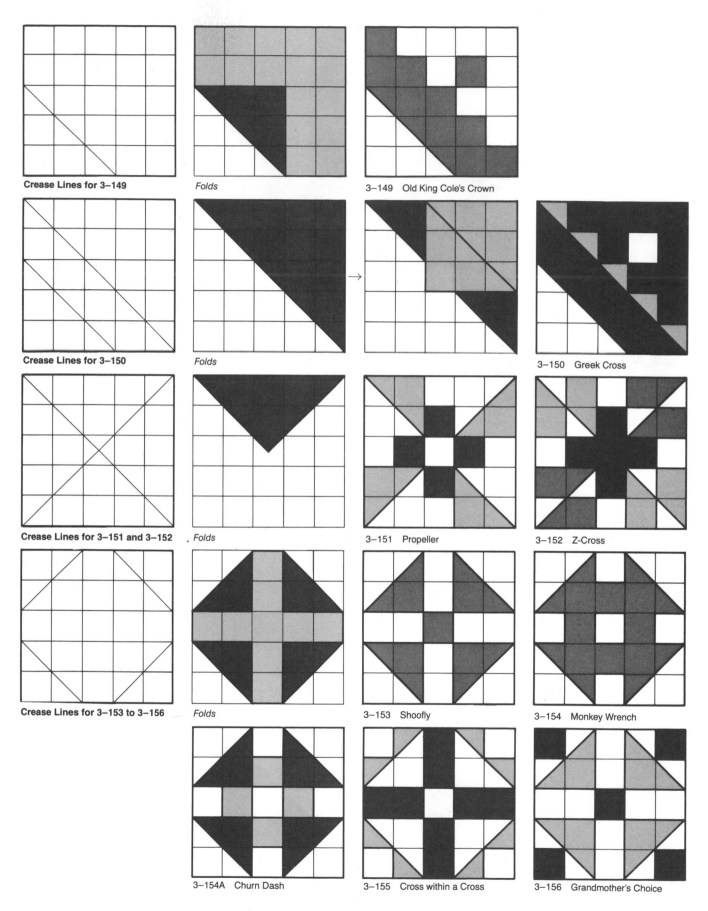

Crease Lines for 3–149

Folds

3–149   Old King Cole's Crown

Crease Lines for 3–150

Folds

3–150   Greek Cross

Crease Lines for 3–151 and 3–152

Folds

3–151   Propeller

3–152   Z-Cross

Crease Lines for 3–153 to 3–156

Folds

3–153   Shoofly

3–154   Monkey Wrench

3–154A   Churn Dash

3–155   Cross within a Cross

3–156   Grandmother's Choice

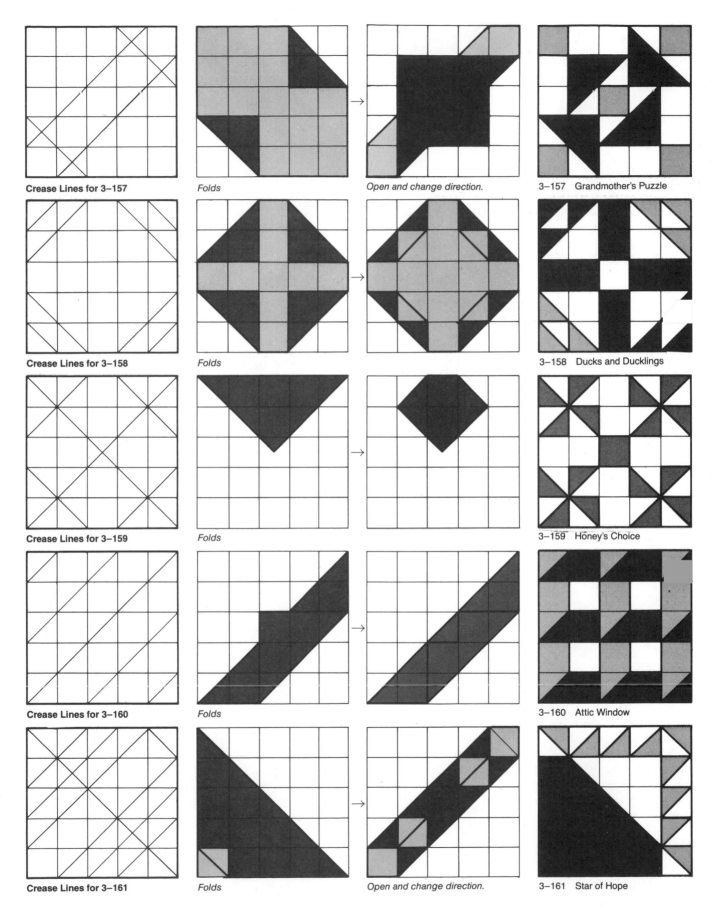

Crease Lines for 3–157 *Folds* Open and change direction. 3–157   Grandmother's Puzzle

Crease Lines for 3–158 *Folds* 3–158   Ducks and Ducklings

Crease Lines for 3–159 *Folds* 3–159   Honey's Choice

Crease Lines for 3–160 *Folds* 3–160   Attic Window

Crease Lines for 3–161 *Folds* Open and change direction. 3–161   Star of Hope

57

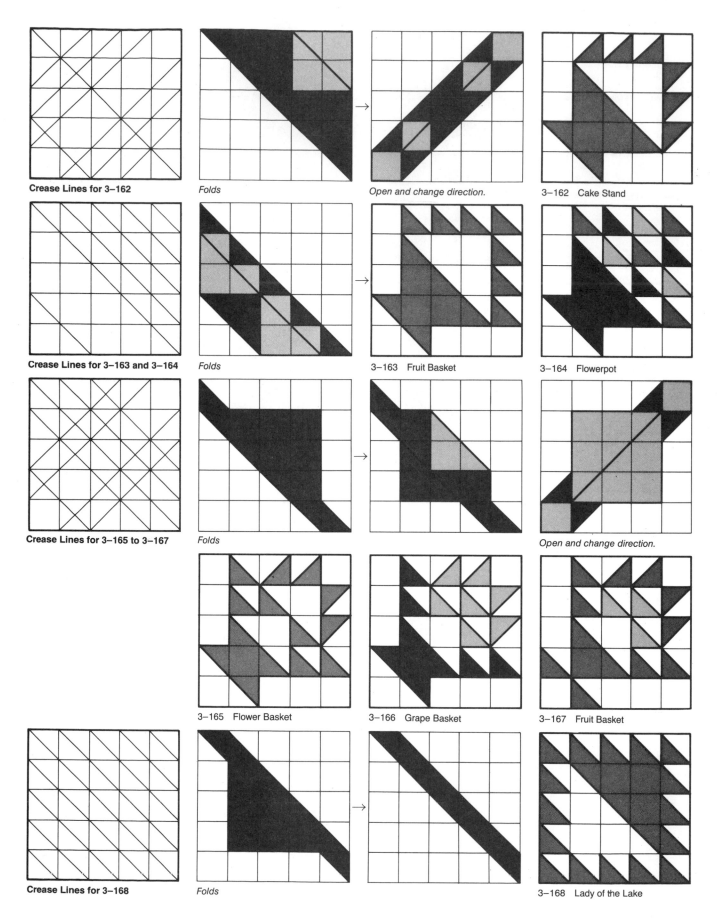

Crease Lines for 3–162

Folds

Open and change direction.

3–162   Cake Stand

Crease Lines for 3–163 and 3–164

Folds

3–163   Fruit Basket

3–164   Flowerpot

Crease Lines for 3–165 to 3–167

Folds

Open and change direction.

3–165   Flower Basket

3–166   Grape Basket

3–167   Fruit Basket

Crease Lines for 3–168

Folds

3–168   Lady of the Lake

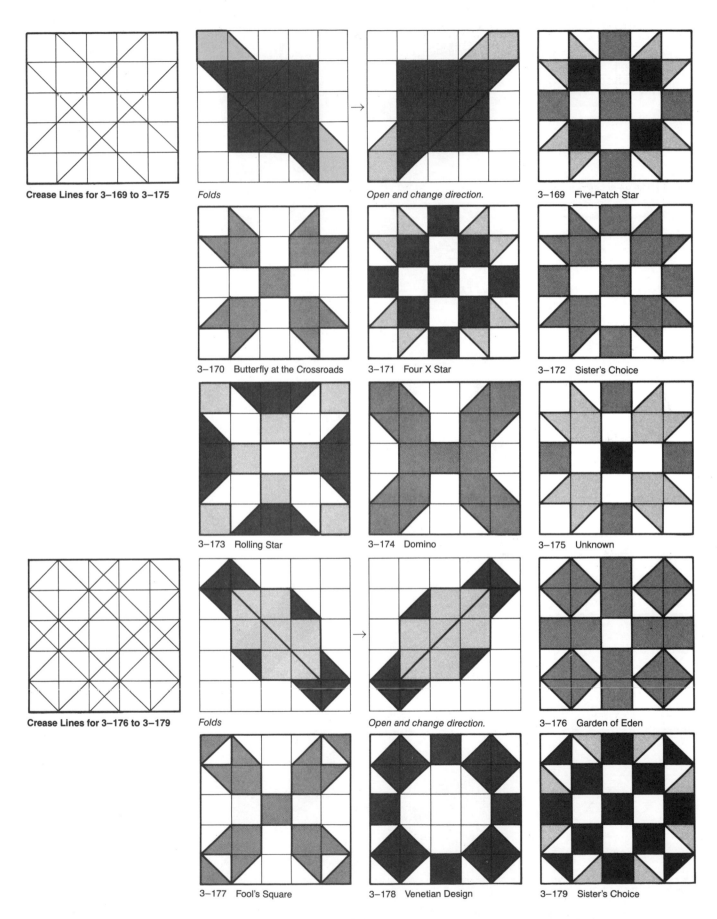

Crease Lines for 3–169 to 3–175

Folds

Open and change direction.

3–169   Five-Patch Star

3–170   Butterfly at the Crossroads

3–171   Four X Star

3–172   Sister's Choice

3–173   Rolling Star

3–174   Domino

3–175   Unknown

Crease Lines for 3–176 to 3–179

Folds

Open and change direction.

3–176   Garden of Eden

3–177   Fool's Square

3–178   Venetian Design

3–179   Sister's Choice

Crease Lines for 3–180 to 3–185

Folds

Open and change direction.

3–180 Wedding Rings

3–181 Flying Geese

3–182 Presentation Quilt

3–183 Old Scraps Patchwork

3–184 Wishing Ring

3–185 Crown and Thorns

Crease Lines for 3–186

Folds

3–186 Double Sawtooth

Crease Lines for 3–187

Folds

3–187 Basket

60

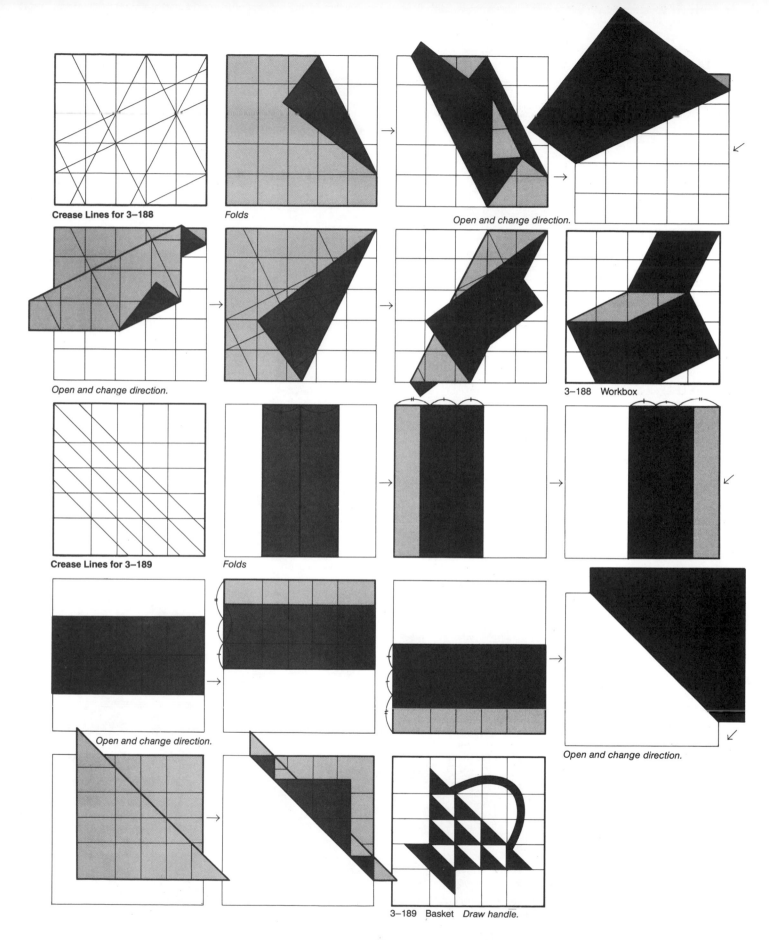

Crease Lines for 3–188

Folds

Open and change direction.

Open and change direction.

3–188 Workbox

Crease Lines for 3–189

Folds

Open and change direction.

Open and change direction.

3–189 Basket   *Draw handle.*

Six-Grid

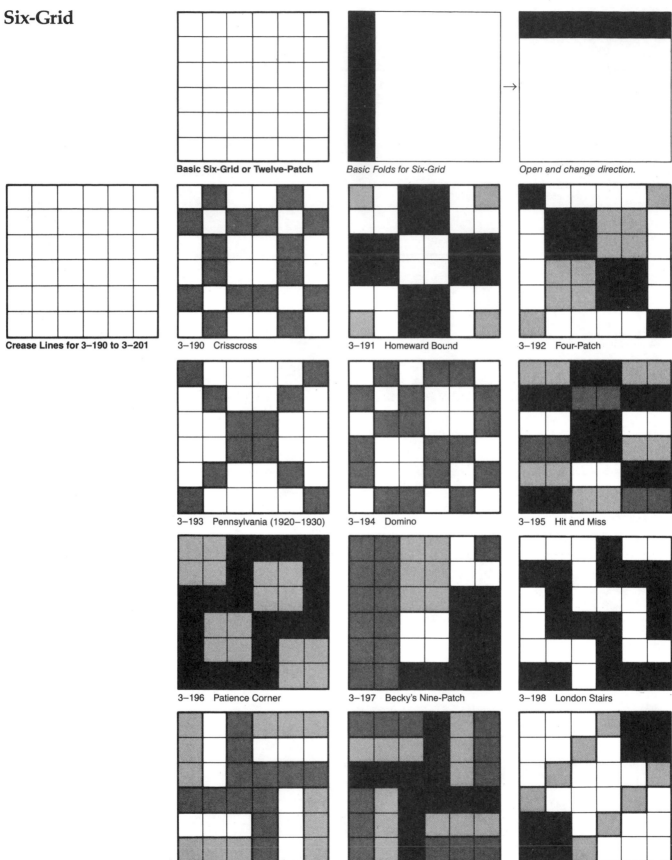

Basic Six-Grid or Twelve-Patch

Basic Folds for Six-Grid

Open and change direction.

Crease Lines for 3–190 to 3–201

3–190 Crisscross

3–191 Homeward Bound

3–192 Four-Patch

3–193 Pennsylvania (1920–1930)

3–194 Domino

3–195 Hit and Miss

3–196 Patience Corner

3–197 Becky's Nine-Patch

3–198 London Stairs

3–199 Propeller

3–200 Spirit of St. Louis

3–201 Double Nine-Patch

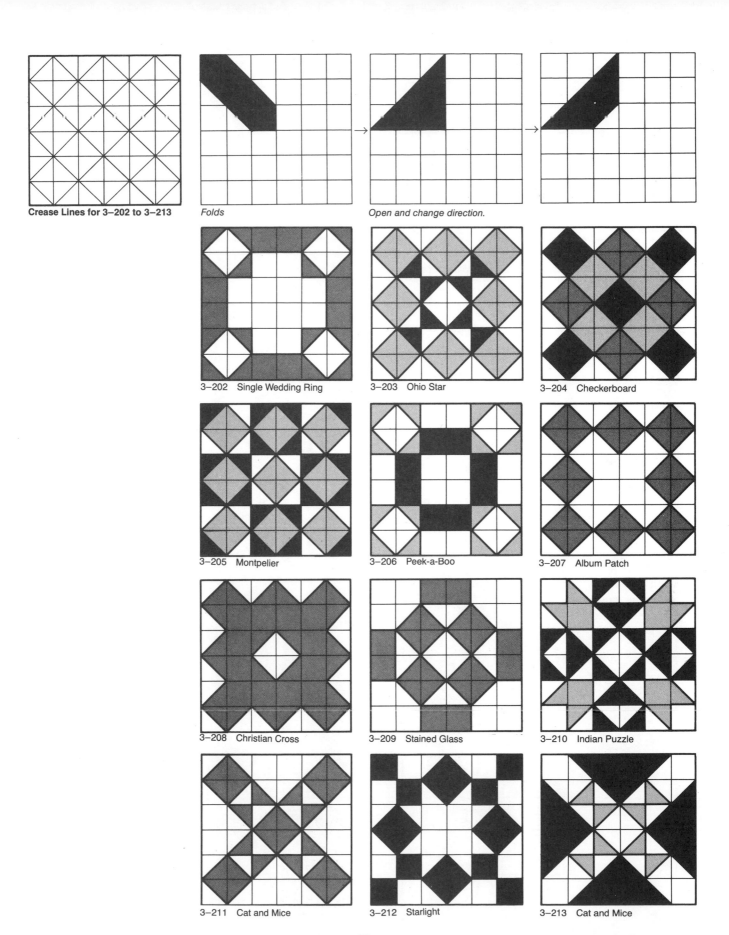

Crease Lines for 3–202 to 3–213

Folds

Open and change direction.

3–202 Single Wedding Ring

3–203 Ohio Star

3–204 Checkerboard

3–205 Montpelier

3–206 Peek-a-Boo

3–207 Album Patch

3–208 Christian Cross

3–209 Stained Glass

3–210 Indian Puzzle

3–211 Cat and Mice

3–212 Starlight

3–213 Cat and Mice

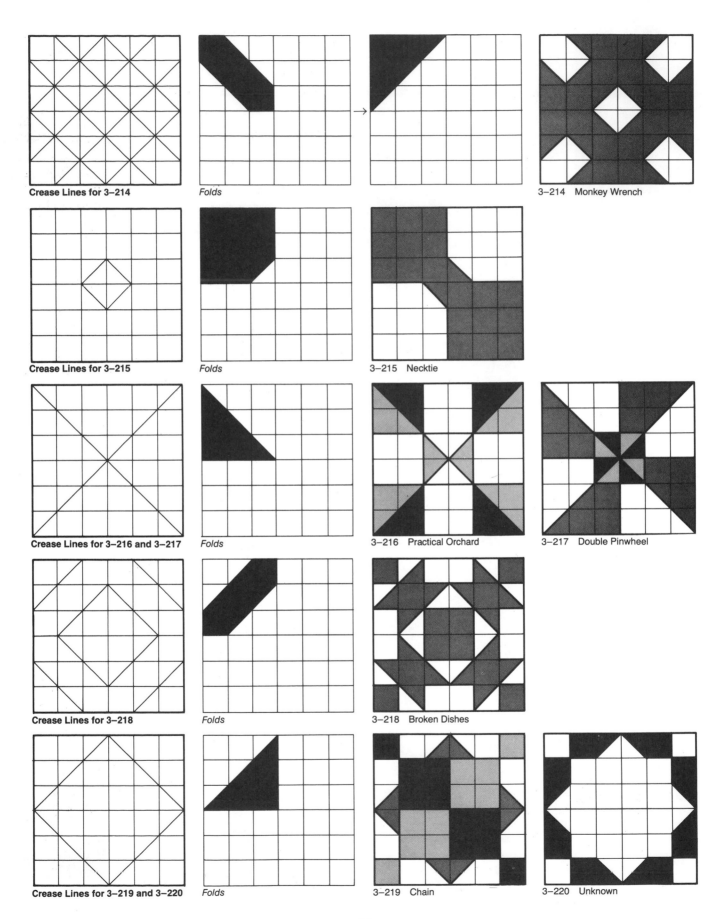

Crease Lines for 3–214 *Folds* → 3–214 Monkey Wrench

Crease Lines for 3–215 *Folds* 3–215 Necktie

Crease Lines for 3–216 and 3–217 *Folds* 3–216 Practical Orchard 3–217 Double Pinwheel

Crease Lines for 3–218 *Folds* 3–218 Broken Dishes

Crease Lines for 3–219 and 3–220 *Folds* 3–219 Chain 3–220 Unknown

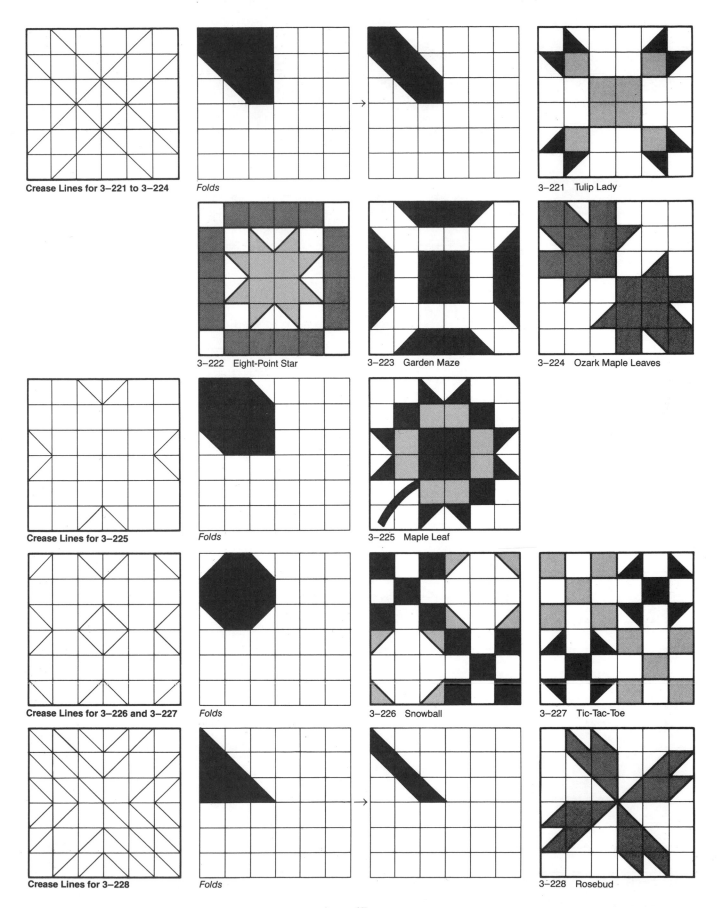

Crease Lines for 3–221 to 3–224

Folds

3–221 Tulip Lady

3–222 Eight-Point Star

3–223 Garden Maze

3–224 Ozark Maple Leaves

Crease Lines for 3–225

Folds

3–225 Maple Leaf

Crease Lines for 3–226 and 3–227

Folds

3–226 Snowball

3–227 Tic-Tac-Toe

Crease Lines for 3–228

Folds

3–228 Rosebud

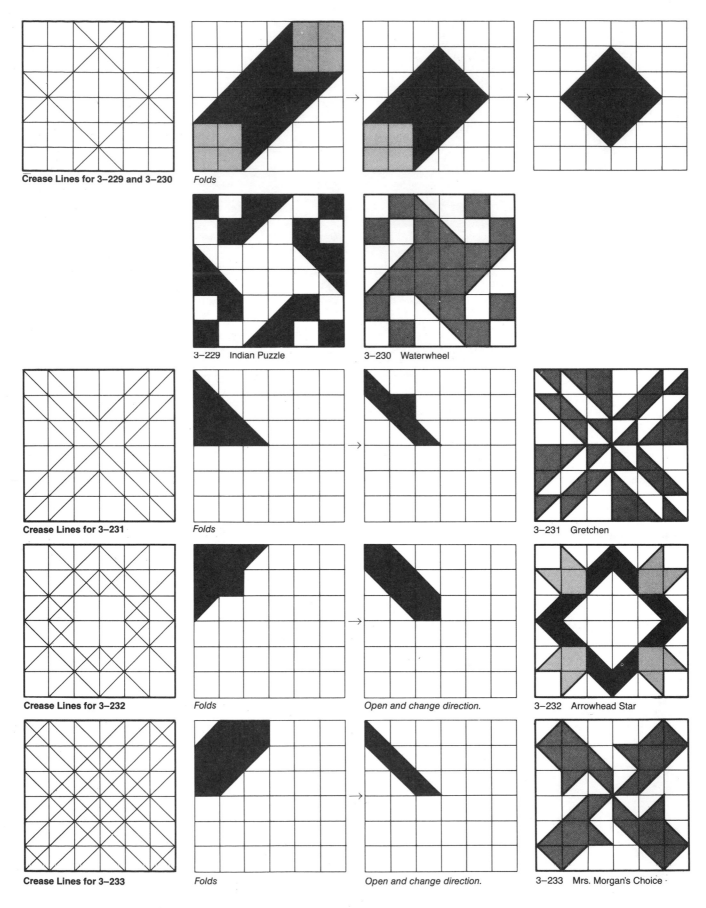

Crease Lines for 3–229 and 3–230

Folds

3–229 Indian Puzzle

3–230 Waterwheel

Crease Lines for 3–231

Folds

3–231 Gretchen

Crease Lines for 3–232

Folds

Open and change direction.

3–232 Arrowhead Star

Crease Lines for 3–233

Folds

Open and change direction.

3–233 Mrs. Morgan's Choice

Crease Lines for 3–234 to 3–237

Folds

Open and change direction.

3–234   Union Square

3–235   Bear's Paw

3–236   Unknown

3–237   Merry Kite

Crease Lines for 3–238 to 3–240

Folds

Open and change direction.

3–238   Eddystone Light

3–239   Capital T

3–240   T Block

Crease Lines for 3–241

Folds

Open last fold.

3–241   Goblet

67

Crease Lines for 3–242

Folds

Open and change direction.

3–242   Mixed T

Crease Lines for 3–243 to 3–246

Folds

Open and change direction.

3–243   St. Gregory's Cross

3–244   Salem

3–245   Block and Stars

3–246   Combination Star

Crease Lines for 3–247

Folds

3–247   St. Louis Star

Crease Lines for 3–248

Folds

3–248   Shadow

68

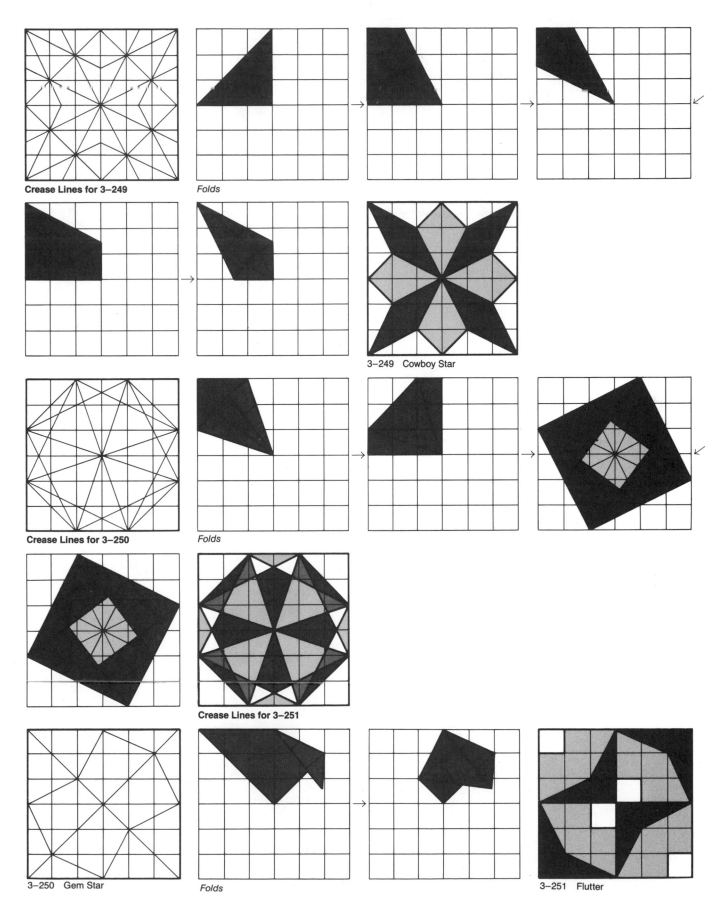

Crease Lines for 3–249

Folds

3–249   Cowboy Star

Crease Lines for 3–250

Folds

Crease Lines for 3–251

3–250   Gem Star

Folds

3–251   Flutter

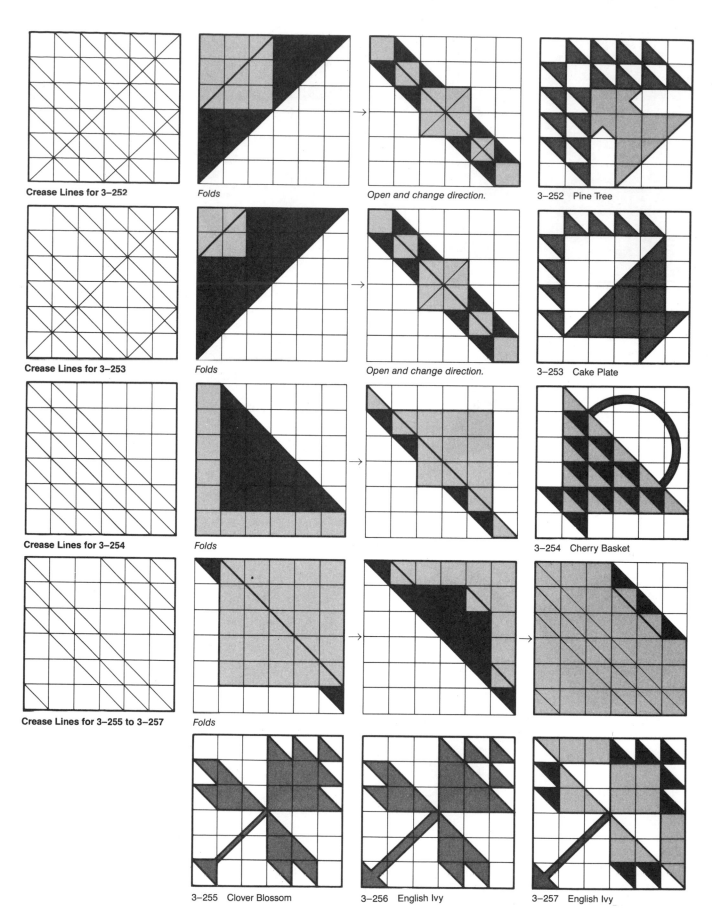

Crease Lines for 3–252

Folds

Open and change direction.

3–252 Pine Tree

Crease Lines for 3–253

Folds

Open and change direction.

3–253 Cake Plate

Crease Lines for 3–254

Folds

3–254 Cherry Basket

Crease Lines for 3–255 to 3–257

Folds

3–255 Clover Blossom

3–256 English Ivy

3–257 English Ivy

Seven-Grid

Basic Seven-Grid

Basic Folds for Seven-Grid

Open and change direction.

Crease Lines for 3–258 to 3–263

3–258   Nine-Patch Variation

3–259   Nine-Patch Variation

3–260   Tonganoxie Nine-Patch

3–261   City Streets

3–262   Stone Mason's Puzzle

3–263   Leavenworth Nine-Patch

Crease Lines for 3–264

Folds

3–264   Lincoln's Platform

Crease Lines for 3–265

Folds

3–265   Birds in the Air

71

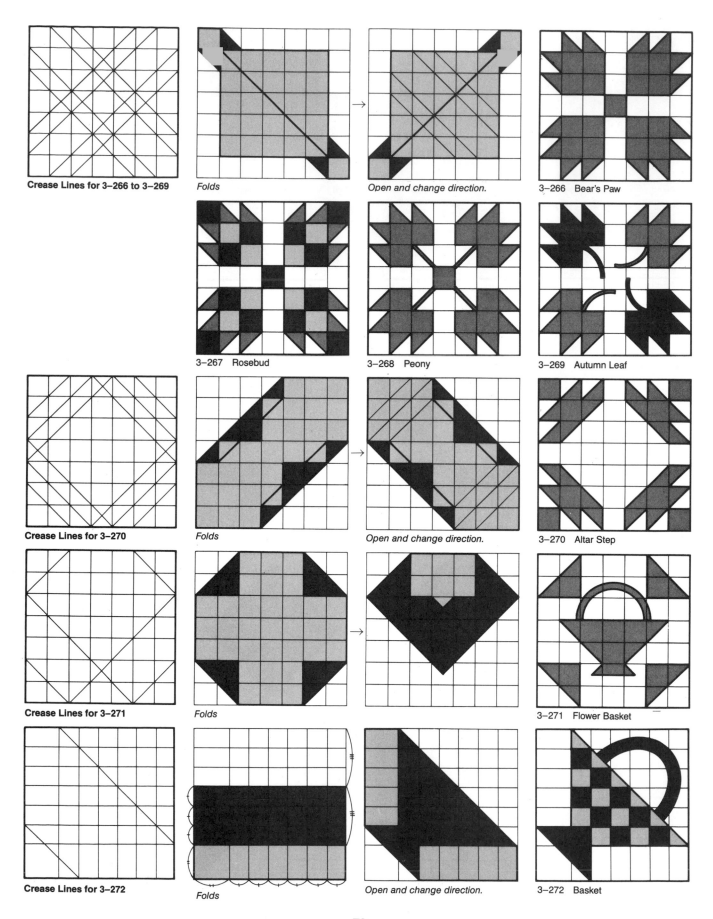

Crease Lines for 3–266 to 3–269

Folds

Open and change direction.

3–266   Bear's Paw

3–267   Rosebud

3–268   Peony

3–269   Autumn Leaf

Crease Lines for 3–270

Folds

Open and change direction.

3–270   Altar Step

Crease Lines for 3–271

Folds

3–271   Flower Basket

Crease Lines for 3–272

Folds

Open and change direction.

3–272   Basket

Eight-Grid

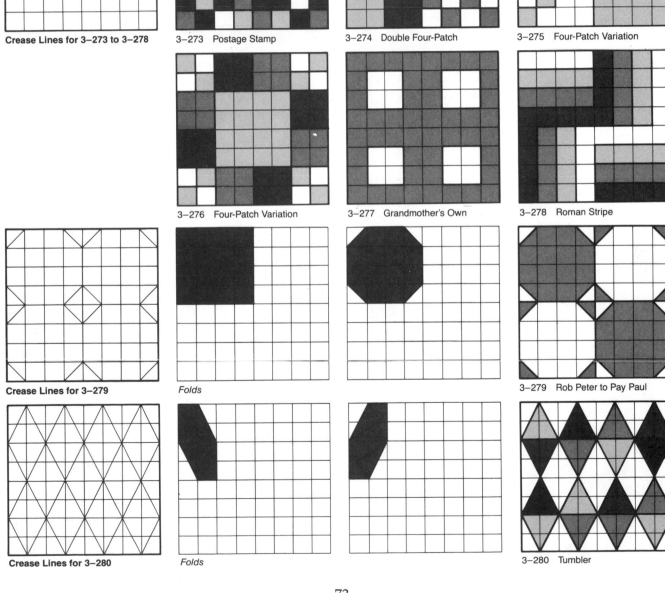

Basic Eight-Grid

Basic Folds for Eight-Grid

Open and change direction.

Crease Lines for 3–273 to 3–278

3–273   Postage Stamp

3–274   Double Four-Patch

3–275   Four-Patch Variation

3–276   Four-Patch Variation

3–277   Grandmother's Own

3–278   Roman Stripe

Crease Lines for 3–279

Folds

3–279   Rob Peter to Pay Paul

Crease Lines for 3–280

Folds

3–280   Tumbler

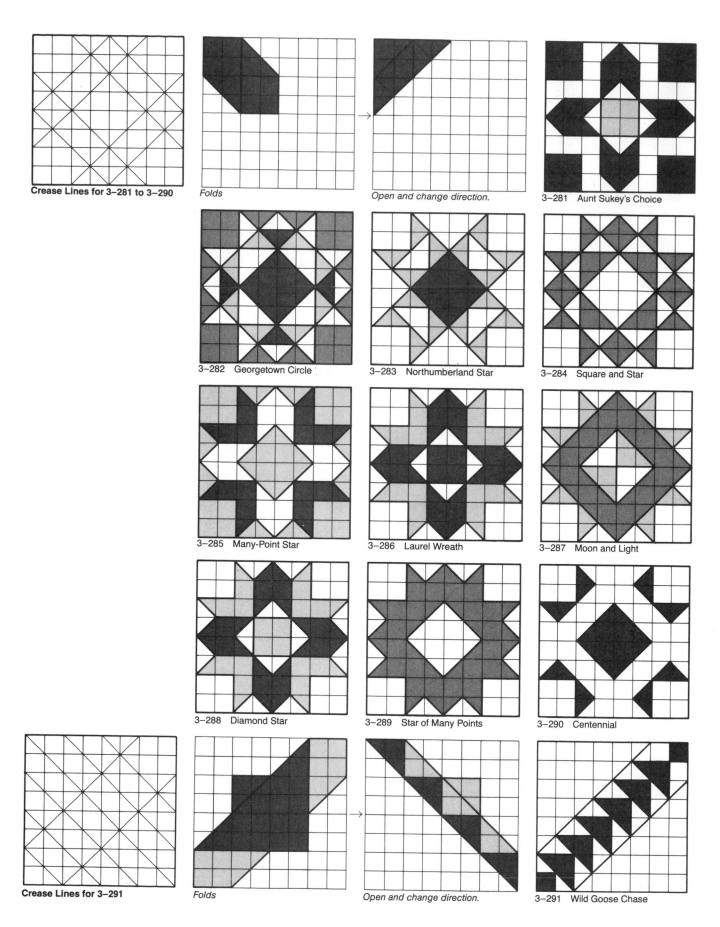

Crease Lines for 3–281 to 3–290

Folds

Open and change direction.

3–281　Aunt Sukey's Choice

3–282　Georgetown Circle

3–283　Northumberland Star

3–284　Square and Star

3–285　Many-Point Star

3–286　Laurel Wreath

3–287　Moon and Light

3–288　Diamond Star

3–289　Star of Many Points

3–290　Centennial

Crease Lines for 3–291

Folds

Open and change direction.

3–291　Wild Goose Chase

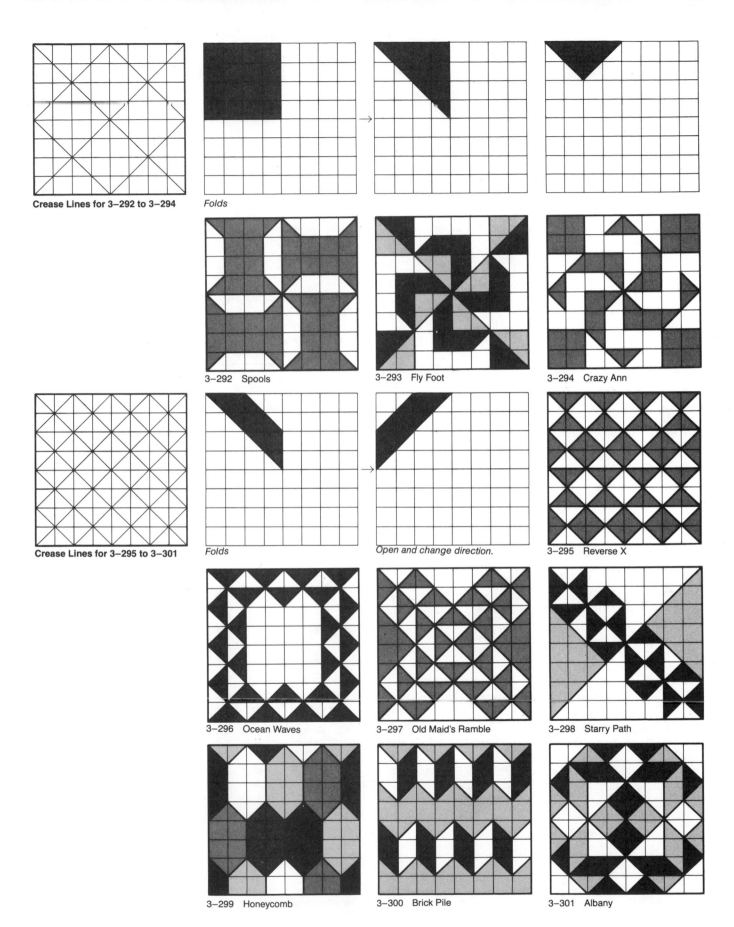

Crease Lines for 3–292 to 3–294

Folds

Crease Lines for 3–295 to 3–301

Folds

Open and change direction.

3–292 Spools

3–293 Fly Foot

3–294 Crazy Ann

3–295 Reverse X

3–296 Ocean Waves

3–297 Old Maid's Ramble

3–298 Starry Path

3–299 Honeycomb

3–300 Brick Pile

3–301 Albany

Crease Lines for 3–302 to 3–304

Folds

Open and change direction.

3–302 Washington Sidewalk

3–303 Album Patch

3–304 Red Cross

Crease Lines for 3–305 and 3–306

Folds

3–305 San Diego

3–306 Odd Fellow's Chain

Crease Lines for 3–307 and 3–308

Folds

3–307 Blindman's Fancy

3–308 Unknown

Crease Lines for 3–309

Folds

Open and change direction.

3–309 Irish Puzzle

76

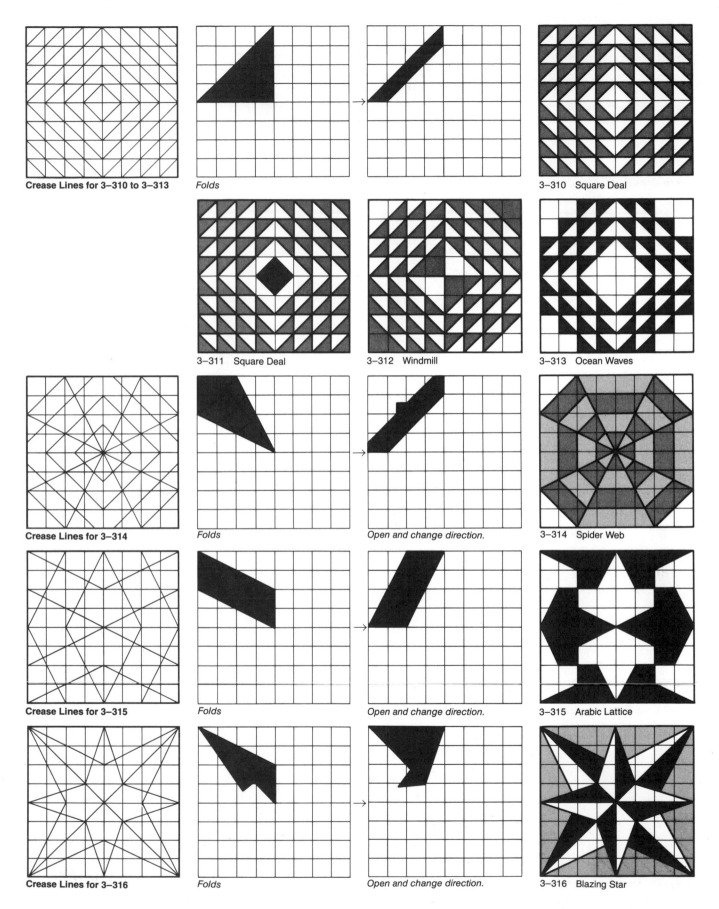

Crease Lines for 3–310 to 3–313

Folds

3–310 Square Deal

3–311 Square Deal

3–312 Windmill

3–313 Ocean Waves

Crease Lines for 3–314

Folds

Open and change direction.

3–314 Spider Web

Crease Lines for 3–315

Folds

Open and change direction.

3–315 Arabic Lattice

Crease Lines for 3–316

Folds

Open and change direction.

3–316 Blazing Star

Crease Lines for 3-317

Folds

Open and change direction.

3-317   Pansy

Crease Lines for 3-318

Folds

Open and change direction.

Open and change direction.

3-318   Rose Quilt

Crease Lines for 3-319 and 3-320

Folds

3-319   Primrose Path

3-320   Pine Tree

Crease Lines for 3-321 and 3-322

3-321   Basket

3-322   Flower Basket

78

Nine-Grid

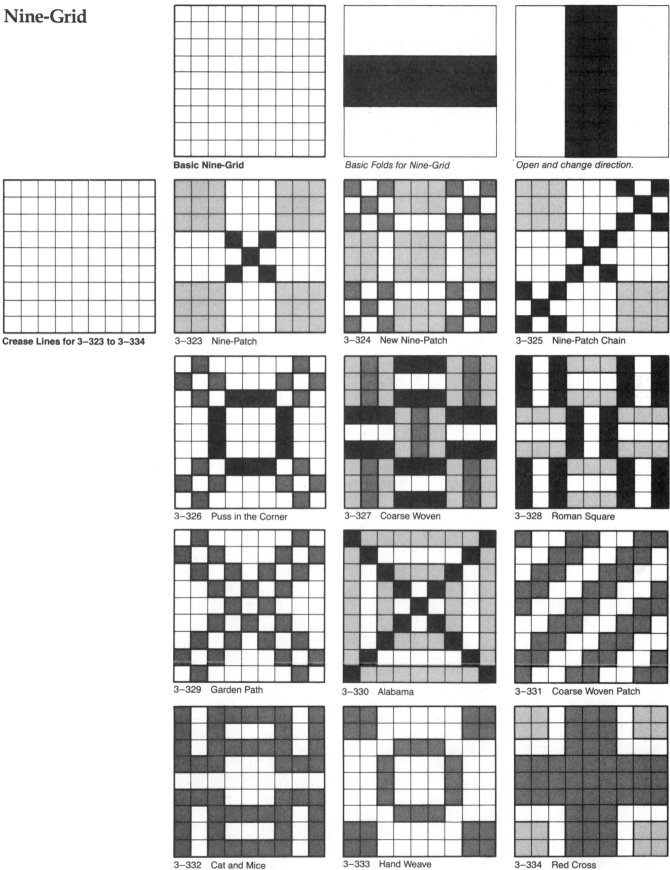

Basic Nine-Grid

Basic Folds for Nine-Grid

Open and change direction.

Crease Lines for 3–323 to 3–334

3–323 Nine-Patch

3–324 New Nine-Patch

3–325 Nine-Patch Chain

3–326 Puss in the Corner

3–327 Coarse Woven

3–328 Roman Square

3–329 Garden Path

3–330 Alabama

3–331 Coarse Woven Patch

3–332 Cat and Mice

3–333 Hand Weave

3–334 Red Cross

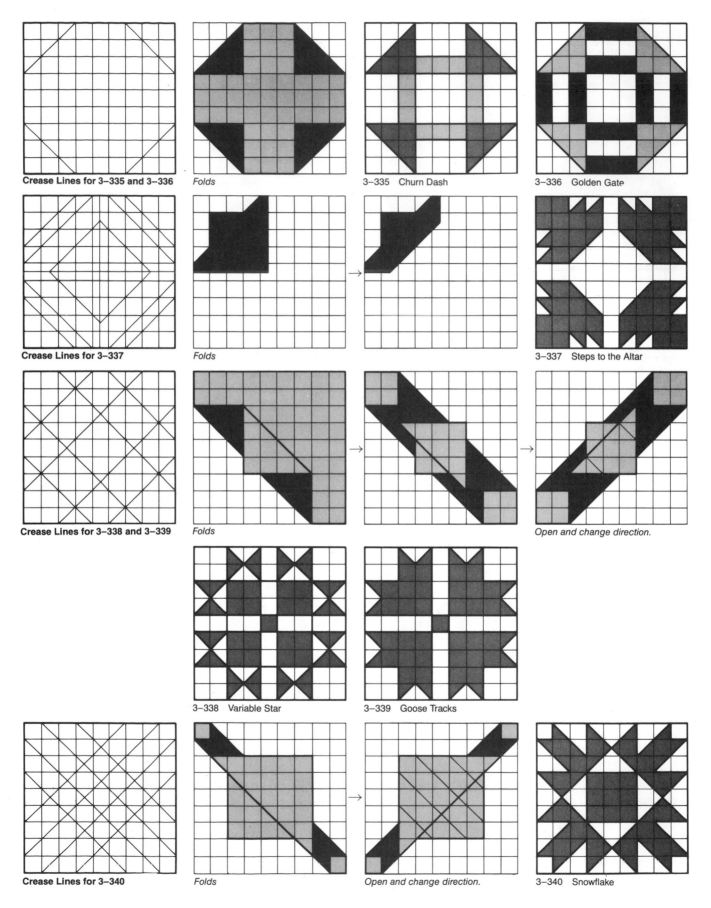

Crease Lines for 3–335 and 3–336

Folds

3–335   Churn Dash

3–336   Golden Gate

Crease Lines for 3–337

Folds

3–337   Steps to the Altar

Crease Lines for 3–338 and 3–339

Folds

Open and change direction.

3–338   Variable Star

3–339   Goose Tracks

Crease Lines for 3–340

Folds

Open and change direction.

3–340   Snowflake

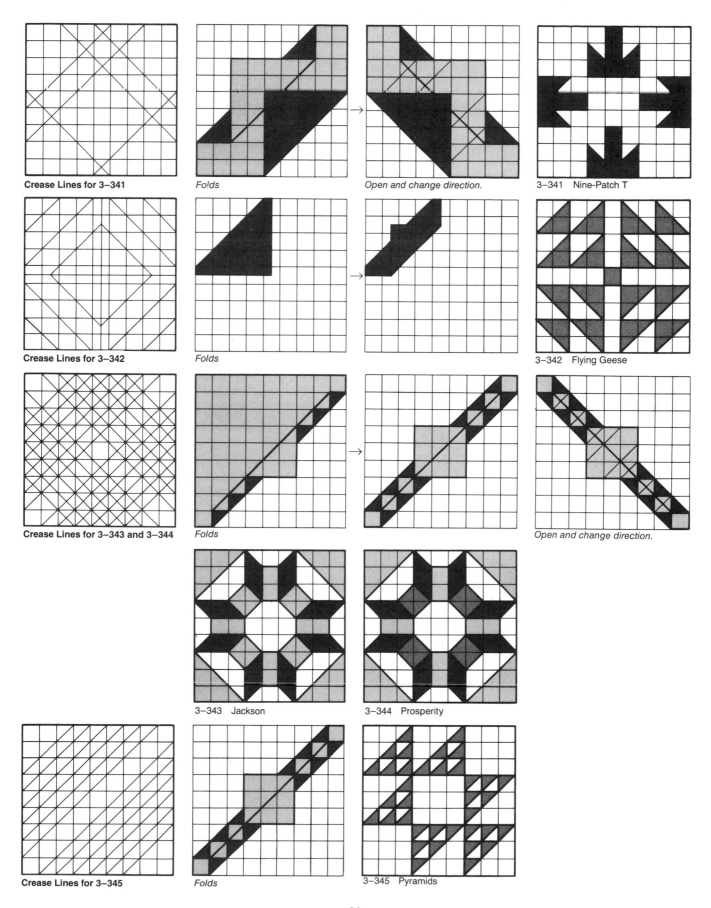

Crease Lines for 3–341

Folds

Open and change direction.

3–341   Nine-Patch T

Crease Lines for 3–342

Folds

3–342   Flying Geese

Crease Lines for 3–343 and 3–344

Folds

Open and change direction.

3–343   Jackson

3–344   Prosperity

Crease Lines for 3–345

Folds

3–345   Pyramids

Log Cabin Variations

Use large paper for the log cabin block. First, bring corner D to corner A, fold corner C to corner D to meet the AB line, and make a crease by folding corner AD to corner BC, and unfold this last fold. Next, fold the center point to meet the crease just made (the vertical line shown).

This will become the center square of the Log Cabin pattern. Divide the vertical line from the new crease line E into four parallel crease lines (F, G, and H), then fold. These will create successively larger squares.

Draw in line extensions as needed for the Log Cabin variation you have chosen.

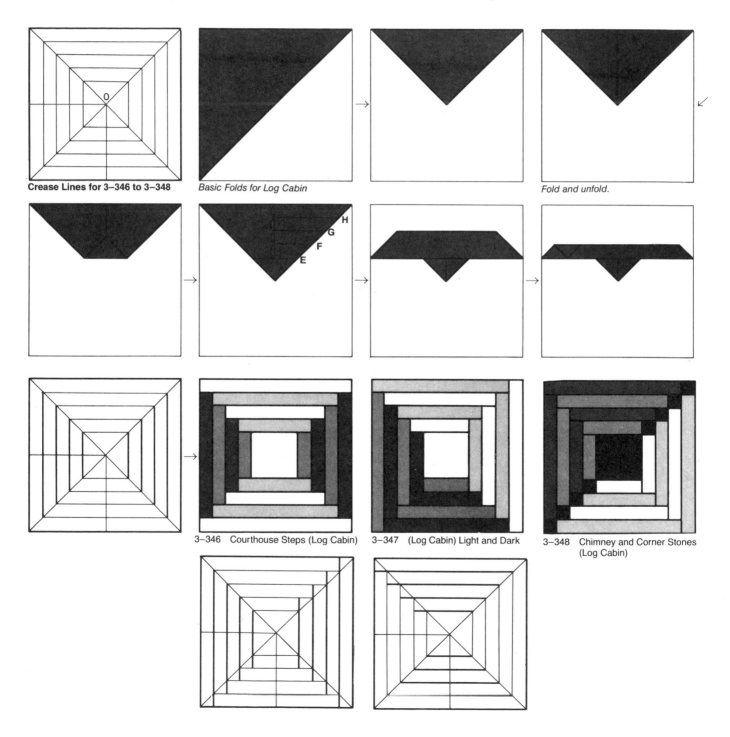

Crease Lines for 3–346 to 3–348

Basic Folds for Log Cabin

Fold and unfold.

3–346   Courthouse Steps (Log Cabin)

3–347   (Log Cabin) Light and Dark

3–348   Chimney and Corner Stones (Log Cabin)

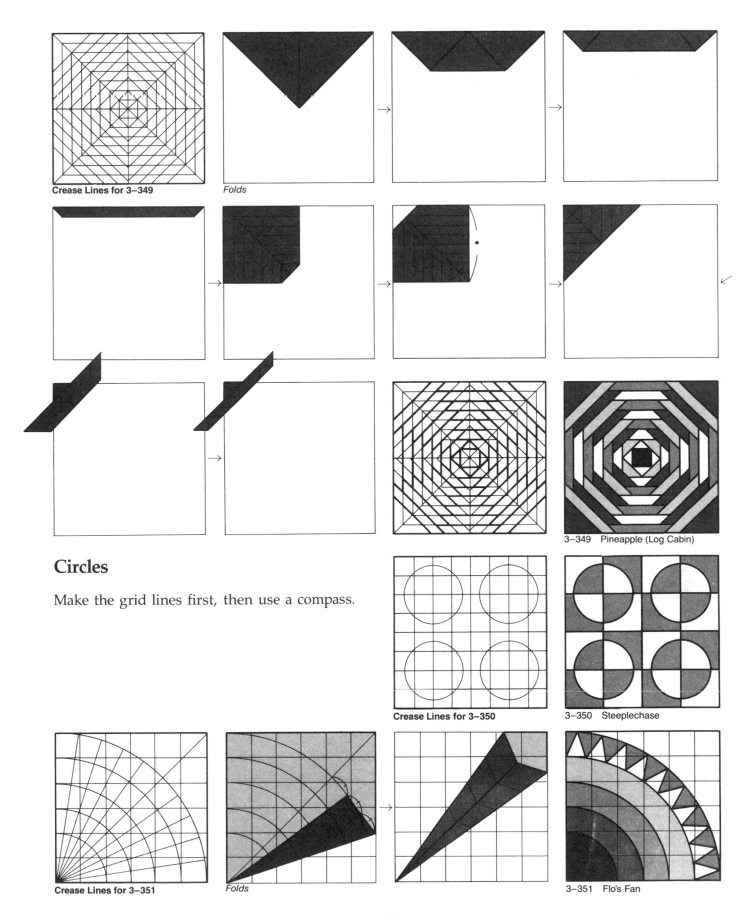

Crease Lines for 3–349

Folds

3–349 Pineapple (Log Cabin)

Circles

Make the grid lines first, then use a compass.

Crease Lines for 3–350

3–350 Steeplechase

Crease Lines for 3–351

Folds

3–351 Flo's Fan

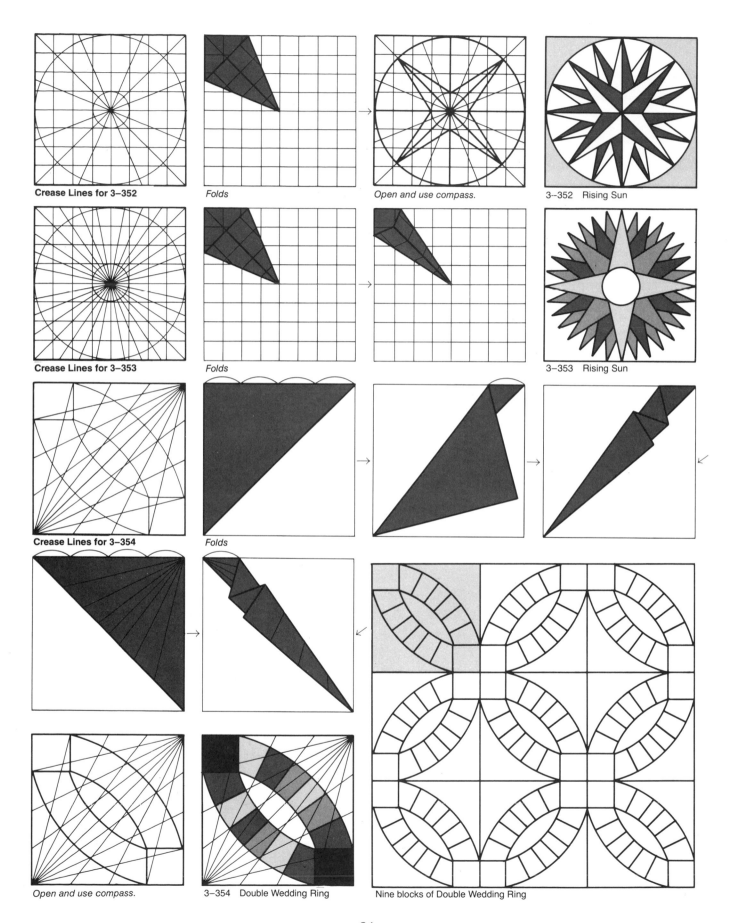

Crease Lines for 3–352

Folds

Open and use compass.

3–352   Rising Sun

Crease Lines for 3–353

Folds

3–353   Rising Sun

Crease Lines for 3–354

Folds

Open and use compass.

3–354   Double Wedding Ring

Nine blocks of Double Wedding Ring

Composition with Two Patterns

Some patterns become a design by combining two different block patterns. These are linked designs, and the number of blocks needed for one quilt must be an odd number, both horizontally and vertically (5 blocks × 7 blocks or 7 blocks × 9 blocks).

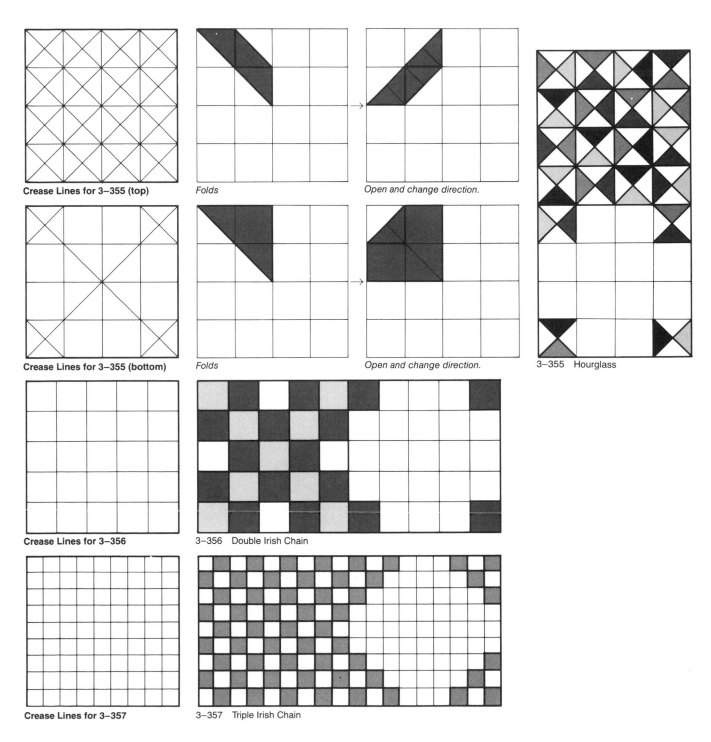

Crease Lines for 3–355 (top)   *Folds*   *Open and change direction.*

Crease Lines for 3–355 (bottom)   *Folds*   *Open and change direction.*   3–355   Hourglass

Crease Lines for 3–356   3–356   Double Irish Chain

Crease Lines for 3–357   3–357   Triple Irish Chain

Triangles

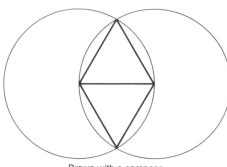

Drawn with a compass

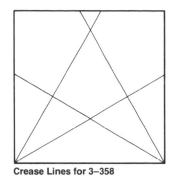

Crease Lines for 3–358

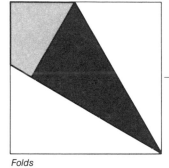

Folds

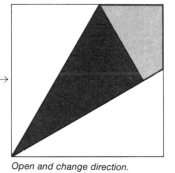

Open and change direction.

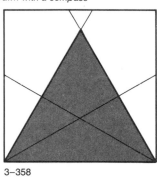

3–358

Pentagons

Crease Lines for 3–359

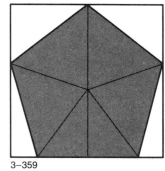

Folds

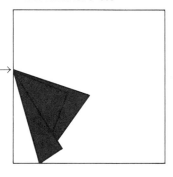

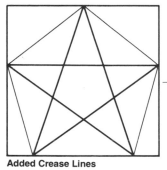

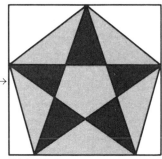

3–359

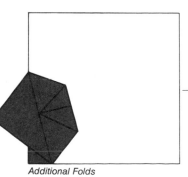

Additional Folds

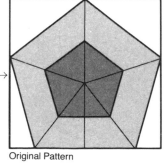

Original Pattern

Added Crease Lines

Original Pattern

86

Hexagons

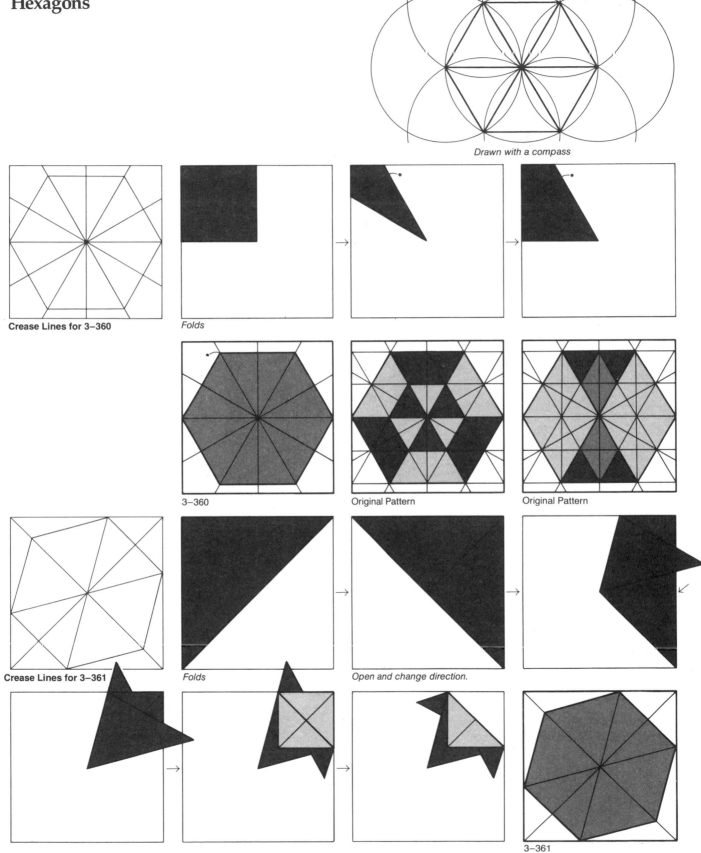

Drawn with a compass

Crease Lines for 3–360

Folds

3–360

Original Pattern

Original Pattern

Crease Lines for 3–361

Folds

Open and change direction.

3–361

Octagons

Crease Lines for 3–362

Folds

Fold two layers.

3–362

Crease Lines for 3–363

Fold papers together.

Open and change direction.

Open and change direction.

Open and change direction.

3–363 Lone Star

Lone Star

88

The same octagon shape can produce different designs depending on the way you fold the origami paper.

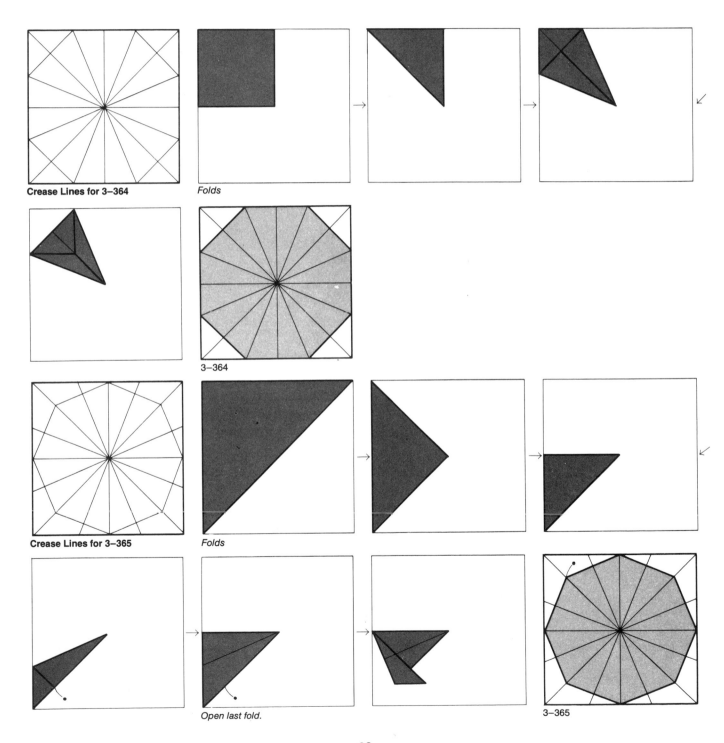

Crease Lines for 3–364

Folds

3–364

Crease Lines for 3–365

Folds

Open last fold.

3–365

4

Hints for Designing Original Quilts

There are many design techniques that will help you create an original quilt. This chapter demonstrates several helpful hints that, used singly or in combination, will make your own designing a breeze.

Changing the Frames of Each Block

When you want to emphasize the block design with only a few blocks, just change the width of the frames in relation to the enclosed block(s) (4–2).

Don't put frames within blocks like window frames, but shift the placement of the central squares. Then you'll have another new design (4–3 and 4–4).

New Patterns from Traditional Pattern Creases

Color the spaces created by folding the traditional pattern creases and try to create a new pattern with new designs.

From creases made for the pattern Rocky Road to Kansas, done with origami folds (see p. 53), color the spaces for the star and the grid alternately, and you will have an optical illusion for a design (4–5).

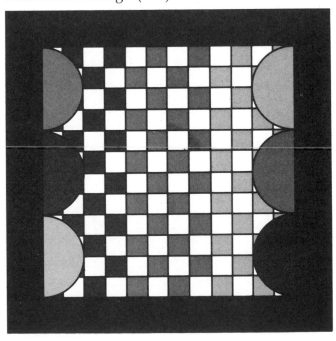

4–1 *Novel framing*

91

Similarly, from the creases for Sister's Choice (p. 59), you can produce a design that will give the impression that you are looking through a stained-glass window (4–6). The image changes if you use a lighter color for the window frames.

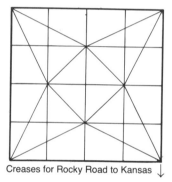

Creases for Rocky Road to Kansas ↓

4–2   4–3   4–4   4–5 Rocky Road to Kansas *variation*

The design in 4–7 is a new pattern made from the creases for Goblet (p. 67), and the design in 4–8 is made from those in Old Maid. Both can become even more interesting by changing the colors and block settings.

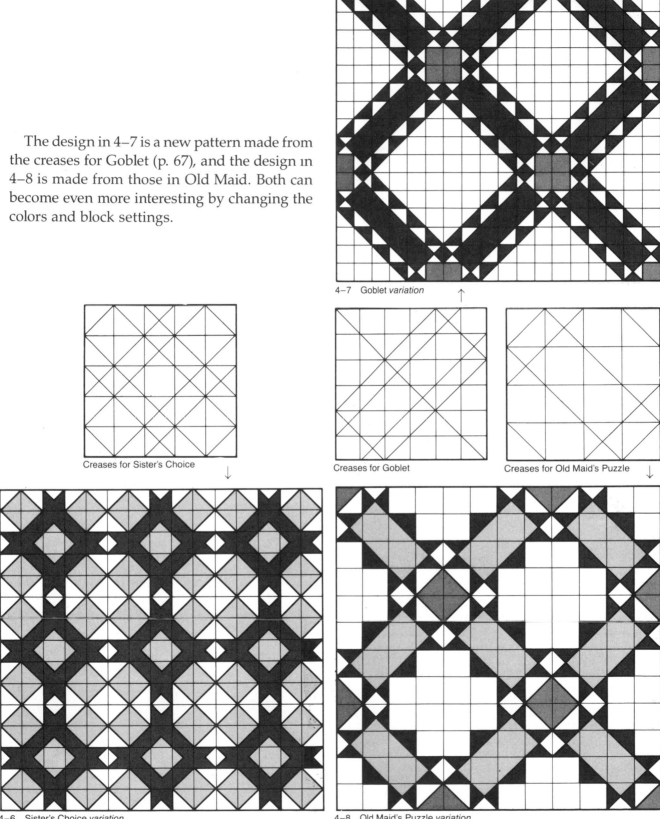

4–7 Goblet *variation*

Creases for Sister's Choice

Creases for Goblet

Creases for Old Maid's Puzzle

4–6 Sister's Choice *variation*

4–8 Old Maid's Puzzle *variation*

4–9 *Design variation*

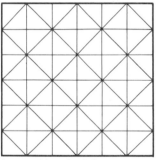

Creases Lines for 4–9

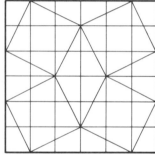

Creases for Roman Style (4–10)

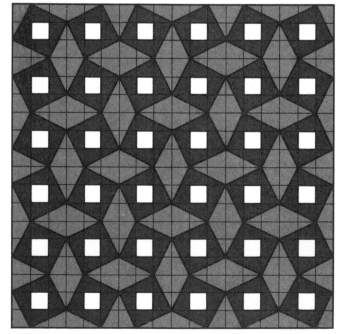

4–10 Roman Style *variation*

Try looking at the creases in 4–9 (p. 63) or in Roman Style (4–10).

Also, see the many possible design variations from a four-grid with three diagonal folds (lines) on p. 111.

Multiple Designs from the Same Crease Lines

How many new designs can you make by using the same creases? Try some with the simple example of a four-grid pattern. From the creases shown in 4–11, use the grid lines and the diagonal lines and color in the spaces with two colors. You can easily make twenty or more new designs with just changes in color. Naturally, if you use more colors, the number of designs will increase. This is a good example of how to produce many designs from simple creases.

Even with the same block pattern, you can juxtapose the blocks in different directions, and you'll have several resulting patterns (4–12). Again, if you make units of four or nine blocks, and change the colors, you will find many other possible combinations. There's no end to the possibilities!

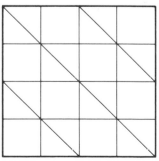

Creases Lines for 4–11

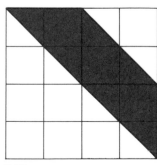

Folds

Multiple Designs from the Same Crease Lines (4–11)

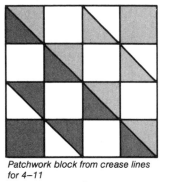

Patchwork block from crease lines
for 4–11

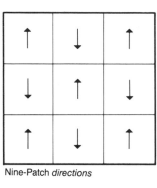

Nine-Patch *directions*

↓   ↓

4–12 *New Design*

A very simple, almost trivial, design can become fresh and alive through a variation in the block setting. On the other hand, it's also true that some designs have fewer and less attractive possibilities than you thought when you first looked at them. You can only find out by folding more origami paper to see which block settings are capable of greater visual impact.

There are so many ways of arranging block patterns, and each one has its own special potential for new and effective combinations. With training, you'll become more skillful in sensing each pattern's possibilities for variation.

As a start, let's place nine blocks of the same pattern in various ways (4–12). As you move them around, you will see which lines can be connected smoothly to another piece and which lines can be connected intermittently. You'll also learn how to create a new continuous pattern by changing colors. Try out some of the examples (4–12 to 4–17).

You'll enjoy the many ways of arranging blocks or changing directions. Just follow the arrows and change the block patterns, and then you don't have to think about the next arrangement. Obviously, some designs are impossible. Consider the Ohio Star pattern for instance; it has the same angle on all four sides. So, unless you change the colors, you cannot change the arrangement. Some patterns, like this one, have a limited number of variations.

There are several ways to juxtapose blocks—by defining a center (4–18 to 4–20) or by connecting blocks diagonally (4–21).

4–13

↑

↑	↓	↑
↑	↓	↑
↑	↓	↑

↑	←	↑
→	↓	→
↑	←	↑

Varied block directions   ↓

4–14

↑

→	←	↑
↑	↓	→
↓	↑	←

→	↑	→
↑	→	↑
→	↑	→

Varied block directions   ↓

4–15

4–16

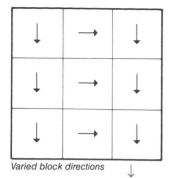

Varied block directions

4-17

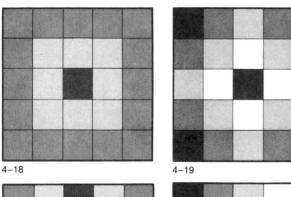

4-18

4-19

4-20

4-21

Off-Center Blocks

Make the star blocks irregularly, but juxtapose them regularly in one direction. Make a continuous line (4–22) with a square unit in the center and four star blocks around it. If you change the direction of the blocks, the line is disrupted and the grid setting the lines cannot be continued. The effect is that of discord, but the pattern has its own kind of charm (4–23).

When set is not only off-centered, but divided irregularly, a continuous line can be made even though the angles are different (4–24).

Altering Sizes

When small blocks become gradually larger, they suggest nearness. When the process is reversed, distance appears to increase (4–25). As the pattern seems to diminish into the distance, it expresses a feeling of depth, and creates an optical illusion (4–2, p. 92).

The squares within the frame are interesting simply because the patterns get larger and larger. But imagine a small flower appliqué on a small block gradually becoming a larger flower on a larger block or a line that continues beyond the frame (4–25). These would also make effective designs.

Let's try to make one. First, fold the origami paper for the number of blocks you would like to use in a diagonal line. Then draw or crease a line from point d of the smallest square to point b of the largest square. The sizes of the squares between are determined by the parallel lines drawn from the marked points on the creases b and c to a side of the frame (4–25).

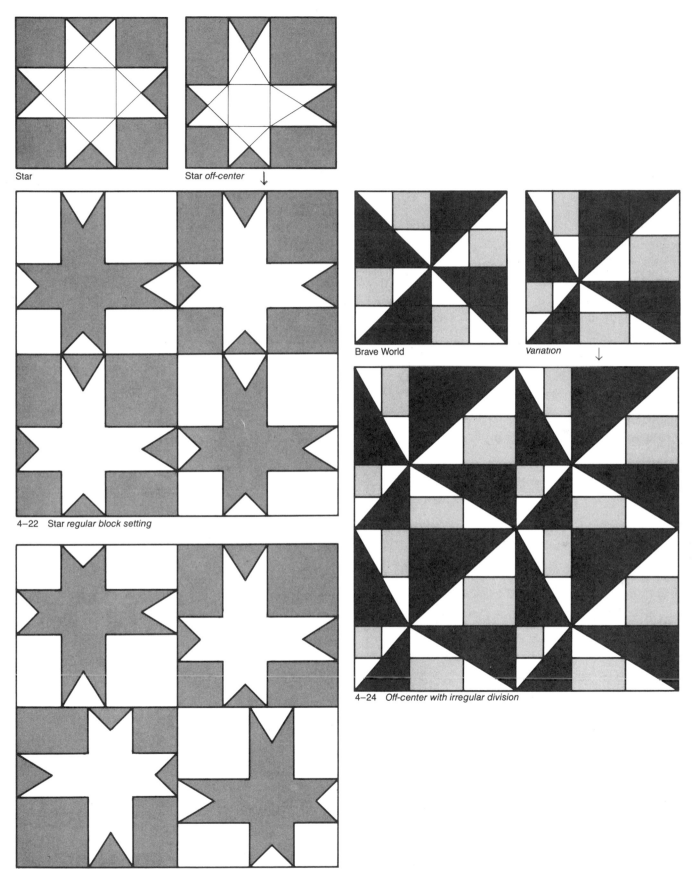

Star

Star *off-center* ↓

4–22 Star *regular block setting*

4–23 Star *altered block setting*

Brave World

Variation ↓

4–24 *Off-center with irregular division*

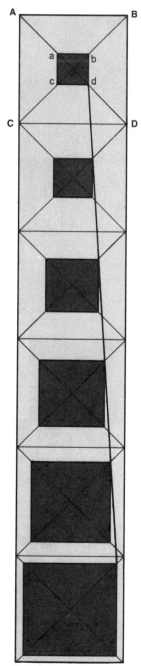

4–25 *Altering sizes*

4–26 *Color contrast*

Color Contrast

If the background color is pale, a darker color will stand out in contrast and suggest a sense of nearness (4–26).

Angles

When a flat block is not connected in a parallel line to another block the same size, the latter block produces a three-dimensional impression, as though the block popped out (4–38 to 4–42, pp. 105–106).

When the design contains only a few pieces, you also increase the impression of speed, but the speed apparently decreases when there are many (4–4, p. 92). Next, shift the blocks within the frame slightly in each block, just by moving them from the left to the right, and a clearer, stronger image will emerge (see 4–3, p. 92).

Curved Lines

Replace the straight line dividing a block with a curved one, and it will give you the sense that you are looking at waves that move (4–27).

Distortion

Distort half a block by one grid, and the continuous line of the pattern will suddenly appear more dynamic (4–28).

Overlapping Images

Overlap two blocks, not completely, but by shifting the top block over one grid vertically and one grid horizontally (see 4–29). This will produce an overlapped design which gives a feeling of thickness. Try this same technique using different colors or by overlapping different patterns. You will see new designs that you never expected (4–29 to 4–32).

4–27 Angles and curved lines

Introducing curves

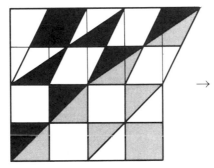 →

4–28 *Distortion*

101

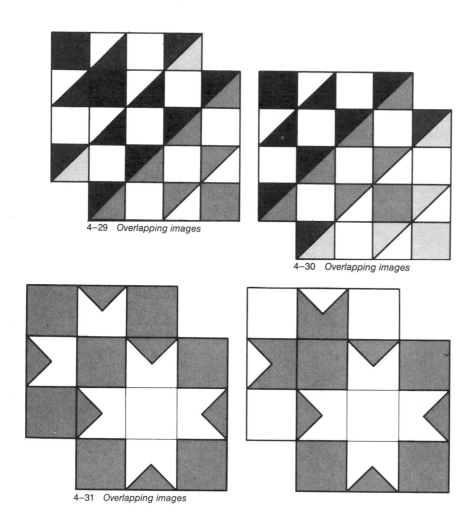

4–29 *Overlapping images*

4–30 *Overlapping images*

4–31 *Overlapping images*

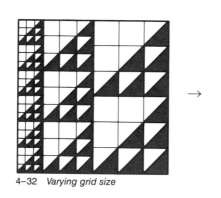

4–32 *Varying grid size*

→

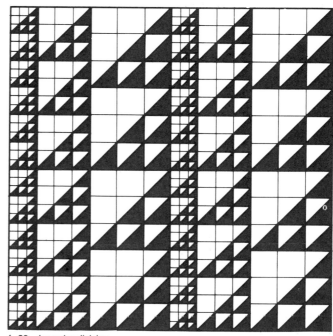

4–33 *Irregular division*

102

Irregular Division

By piecing small blocks to large blocks (4–33), you achieve the effect shown opposite. By making the grid smaller or larger, they become vivid and alive, supplying a sense of movement (4–33).

Light and Dark Effects

Spools is an old pattern. It may be interesting to adapt a New York Fireplug as a creative design. The same shapes juxtaposed in light and dark can create an optical illusion design (4–34 and 4–35).

Doubled Images

A block made with the same shapes in different sizes and using a gradation in colors can be a quite effective design when patched together (4–36). The larger the gap in color gradations, the sharper the image.

You may get many hints from some woven patterns, like the pattern called woven, which uses blocks with continuous designs (4–37).

Diamonds

When a diamond made in an octagon or a hexagon is equally divided in accordance with the grid division, lines of different angles are created which produce a surprising effect as a design. Use large origami paper, and try some variations from traditional patterns.

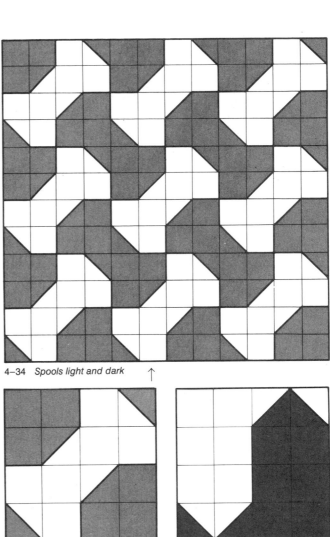

4–34   Spools light and dark   ↑

Spools

New York Fireplug   ↓

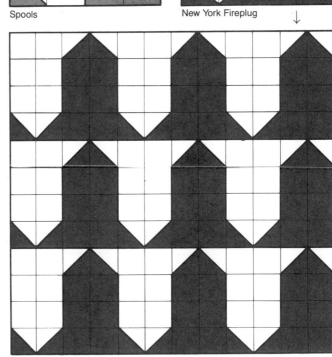

4–35   New York Fireplugs *light and dark*

103

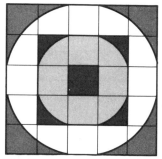

Triple Square and Double Circle ↓

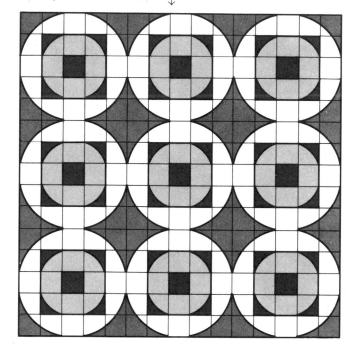

Diamonds in an Octagon

You can use diamond shapes to create a dynamic eight-point star, made by the repetition of four quarter blocks. Count this as one block, and draw division lines in the corners as you would on the square block. You'll find an incredible number of variations that increases when you use different colors (4–38). Again, if blocks are placed with gradually changing angles, you alter the field of vision and create an optical illusion which provides a sense of speedy movement.

Weaving variation

Weaving variation

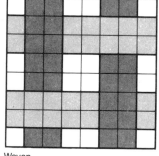

Woven

→

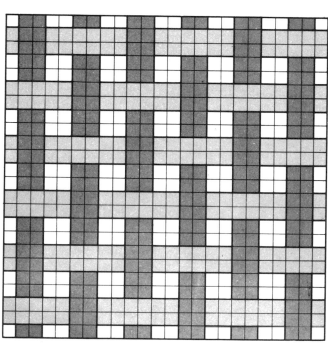

4–37 Woven *design*

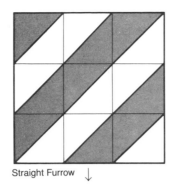

Straight Furrow ↓

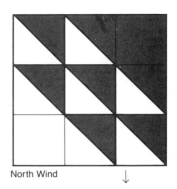

North Wind ↓

4–38 Eight-Point Star *design*

4–39 Eight-Point Star *design*

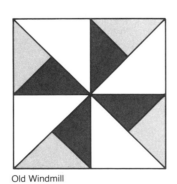

Old Windmill

 →

4–40 Eight-Point Star *design*

105

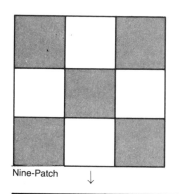

Nine-Patch

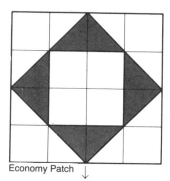

Economy Patch

4–41 Diamonds (eight-point star) *variation*

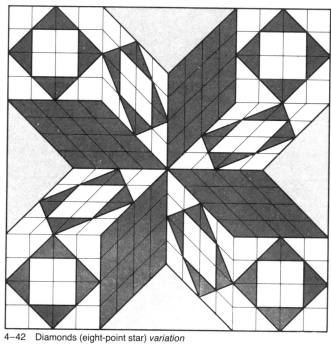

4–42 Diamonds (eight-point star) *variation*

Diamonds in a Hexagon

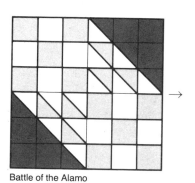

Battle of the Alamo

4–43 *Hexagon diamonds*

Farmer's Puzzle ↓

Sister's Choice ↓

4-44 *Hexagon diamonds*

4-45 *Hexagon diamonds*

Diamonds in a Hexagon

Equal division of one side of a diamond shape can be made by cutting a diamond shape, then marking the division lines on that shape only. Then elongate the lines toward the sides parallel to them (4-43 to 4-47).

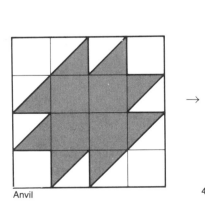

Anvil

→

4-46 *Hexagon diamonds*

Mosaic

4–47 *Hexagon diamonds*

Parallelograms

The parallelogram pattern made of three different angles (4–48) is especially interesting as a three-dimensional design. When you fit other patterns into this design, the impact can be rather startling.

New Images

The design hints that follow are for those who want to make something strikingly new, something modern and highly technical, or something that resembles Art Deco. You can use simple but effective designs without getting into complex patterning.

Parallelogram

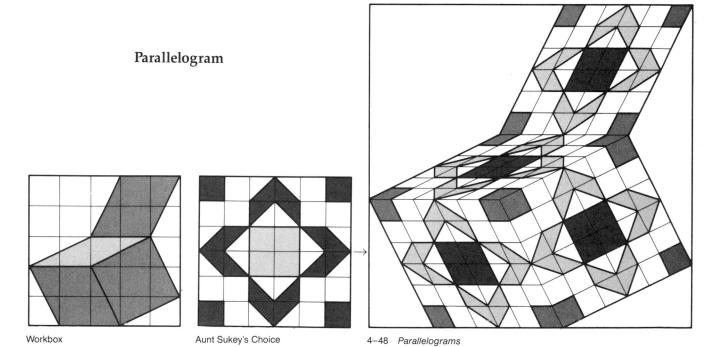

Workbox

Aunt Sukey's Choice

4–48 *Parallelograms*

Art Deco and Computer Images

In the 1920s and 1930s, the new style of interior design, Art Deco, became very popular in Europe and America. This new era for design avoided redundant lines and simplified images with a new sense of color. These types of images also affected quilt design.

Let's try to make something that's your own highly technical design (4–49 to 4–56), not simply an imitation of Art Deco. Computer graphics have also altered our design conceptions. Some of these patterns reflect those image possibilities.

Three-Dimensional Images

Three-dimensional designs that offer a sense of depth and height are well suited to our modern, technological age. Shade gradations between light and shadow and a simple block motif can produce a sharp, highly technical design made with only simple lines (4–57 to 4–68).

Art Deco

4–49 *Typical computer image*

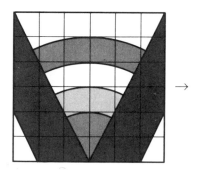

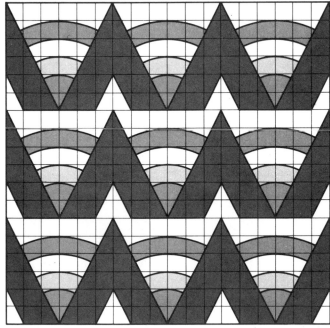

4–50 *Classic Art Deco*

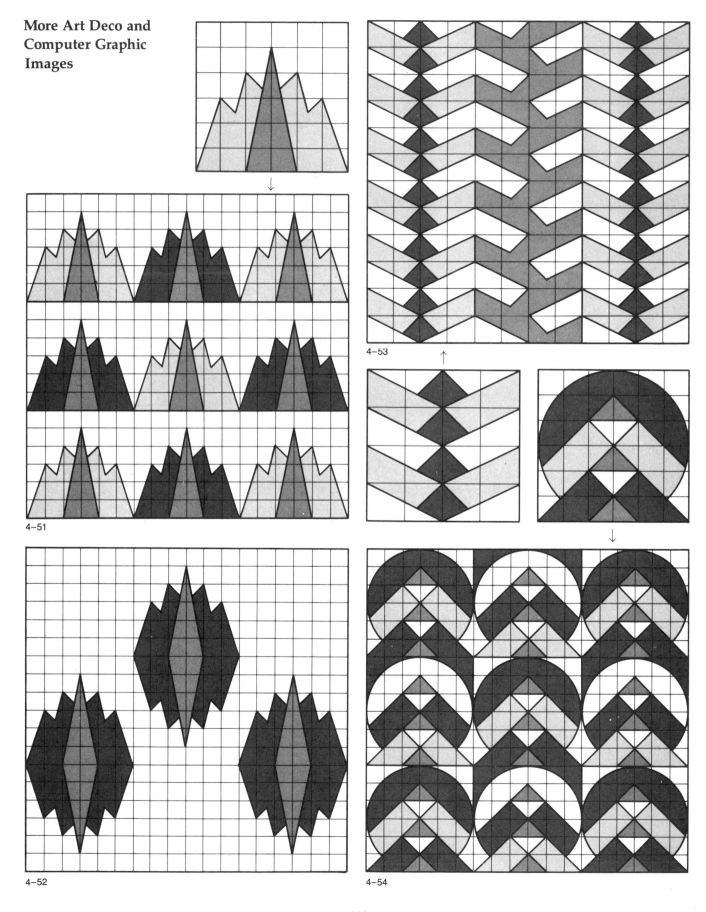

4–51

4–52

4–53

4–54

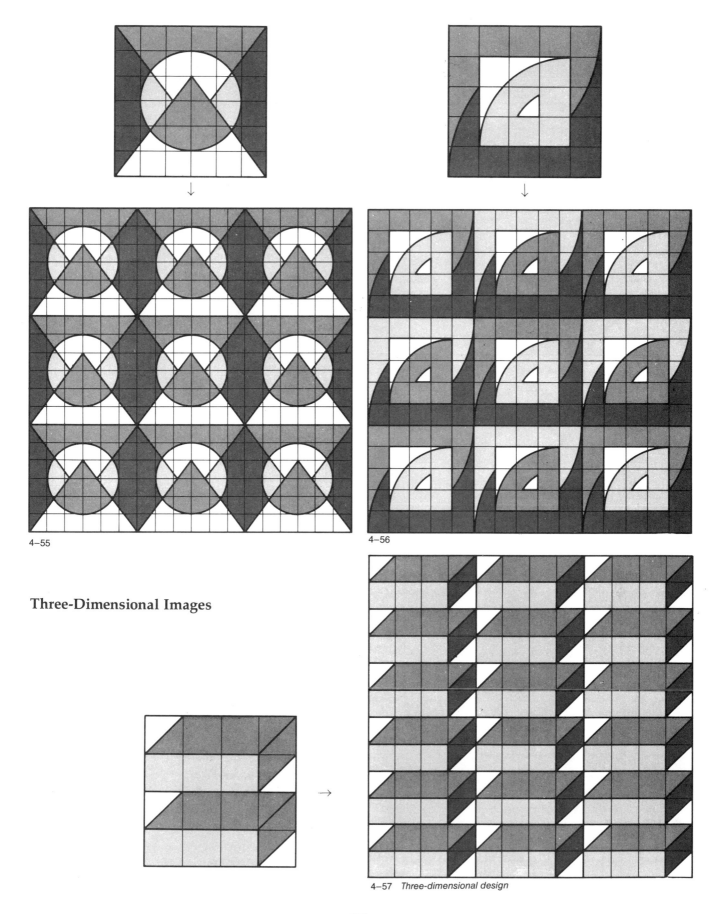

4–55

4–56

Three-Dimensional Images

4–57 *Three-dimensional design*

111

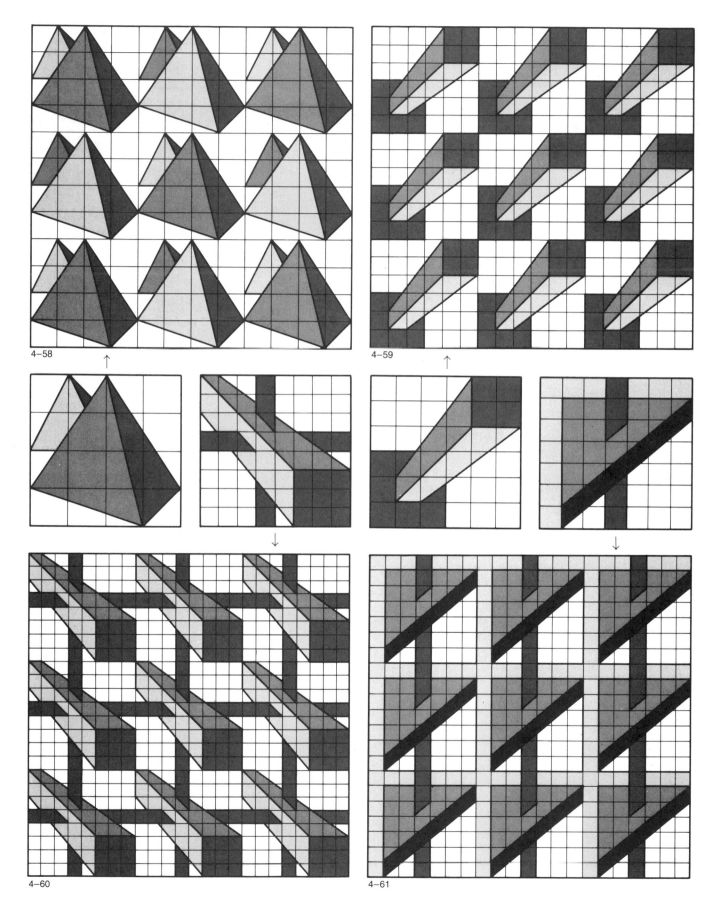

4–58

4–59

4–60

4–61

112

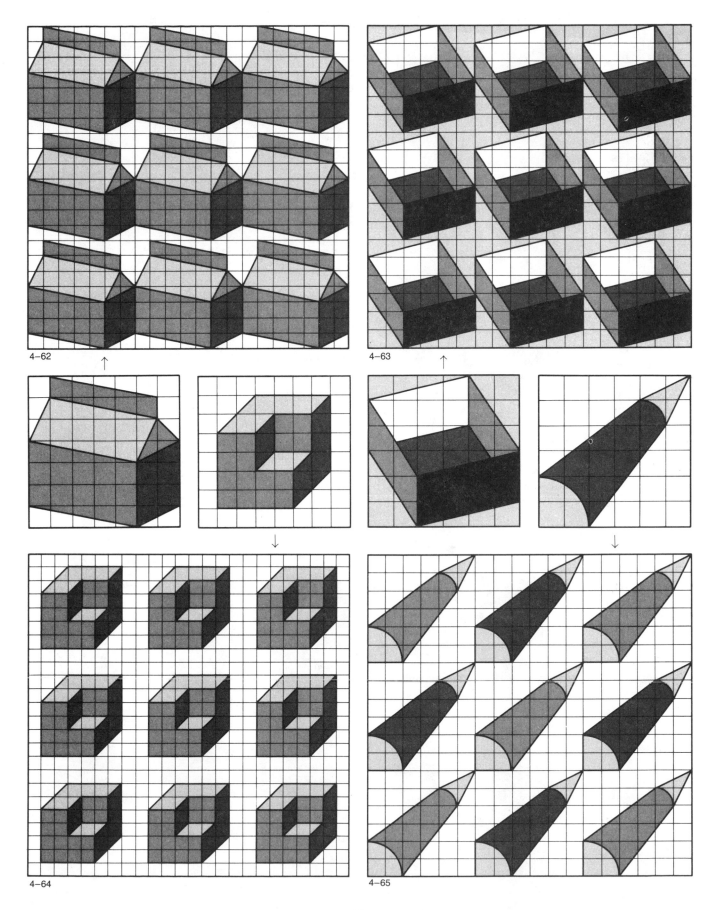

4-62

4-63

4-64

4-65

113

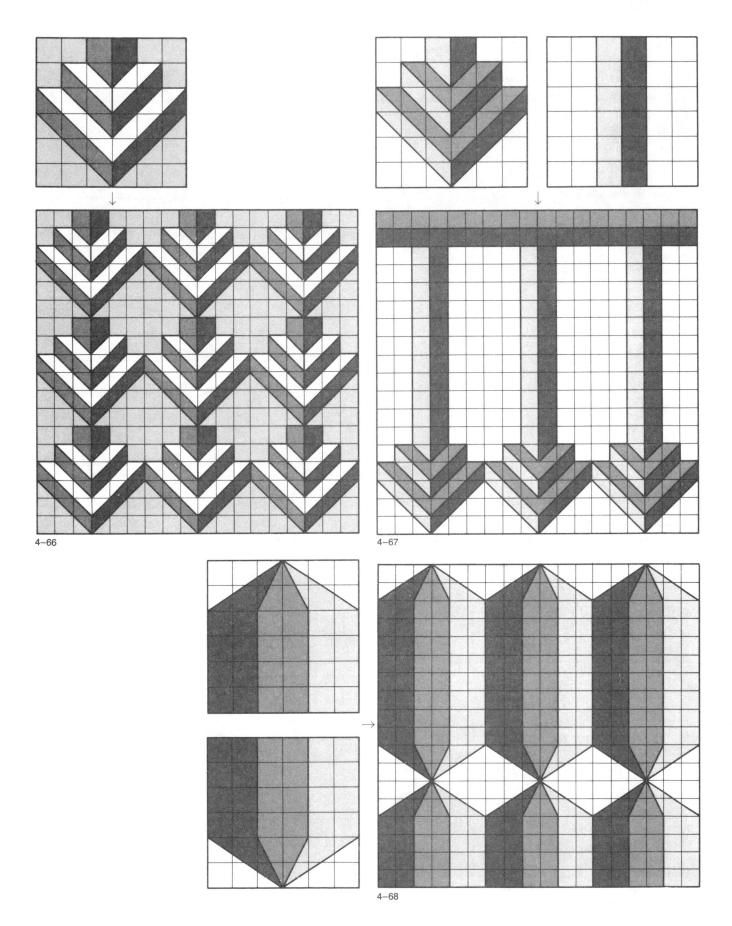

4-66

4-67

4-68

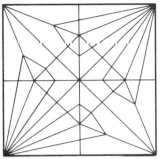

Crease Lines for 4–69 to 4–71
Origami Crane
(traditional step 7 folded and opened)

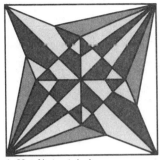

4–69 *Abstract design*

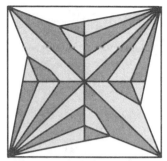

4–70 *Abstract design*

Abstract Designs

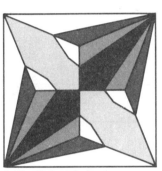

4–71 *Abstract design*

Abstract Designs

If you open up folded origami objects, you'll find that crease lines make fascinating designs.

Take the origami crane, for example, color the spaces made (before folding the head and tail), and you'll discover a surprisingly new abstract design (4–69 to 4–71).

Striped Designs

Make the creases in the origami with enough width for stripes and color them in various ways. These will give you an idea about the balance between the color and the width. It is even simpler if you just cut many colored origami into many different widths.

Even in the case of the traditional Log Cabin pattern, if you change the width of the stripes, you can simplify the method for making the design. In this way, the design becomes quite modern. If you cut the combined stripes in a circle (4–72), or just add some other pieces to disrupt the balance, the image becomes totally different (4–73 and 4–74).

Striped Designs

4–72 *Striped design*

4–73 *Striped design*

4–74 *Striped design*

5

Block Setting Using Origami

Quilts are usually made by assembling blocks. When the blocks are placed side by side, a whole design emerges that seemed unimaginable when just looking at only one block.

When you see the same posters one after another on a wall, the image is strongly emphasized, and sometimes even startling. In the 1960s, Andy Warhol created shocking painted images by juxtaposing pictures of Campbell's Soup cans, or portraits of Marilyn Monroe, in a way not seen before in the visual arts.

The fun of quilt making, which captivates many people, is the discovery of the totally unexpected effect that can be achieved by arranging continuous blocks. Furthermore, the way of arranging blocks, a change in color, or the use of different prints, will produce endless variations that only become evident when all the parts are finally put together.

The pattern, Streak of Lightning, is made with a three-patch block, but the way these three-patch blocks are placed creates a continuous design. When you position nine blocks a certain way, you can create two continuous zigzag lines (5–1). You can make a zigzag design even if you use different pieces of cloth for the central grid.

The simplest of the nine-patch patterns has a beauty of its own, even when only two colors are used. The setting in 5–2 is made of two kinds of nine-patch blocks. The checkerboard design 5–3 is made with nine-patch blocks juxtaposed diagonally. As this design shows, if one side of the quilt is made with seven blocks, the design will have twenty-one diagonal lines. If you use gradations in color or prints, or different kinds of cloth, the design will be even more interesting.

Shoofly can be made with many kinds of prints in the center square (5–4). Try different color schemes, such as using the same color in the central piece, or using many different prints for the triangular pieces (5–5). In this way, you can develop an idea for coloring the quilt as a whole.

Here are some combinations of origami block

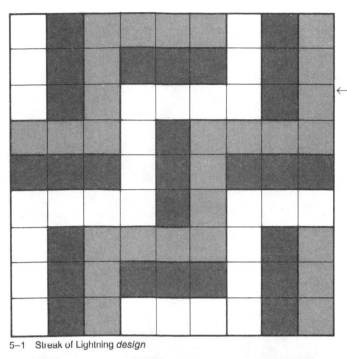

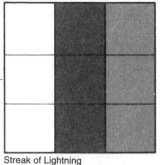

Streak of Lightning

5–1 Streak of Lightning *design*

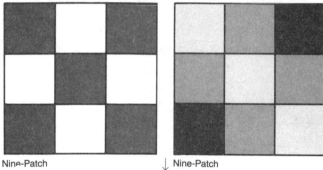

Nine-Patch   ↓ Nine-Patch

5–2 *Two* Nine-Patch *block combinations*

settings. Looking at the examples in these pages, it may strike you that they seem much like computer graphics, since the designs change instantly with the setting or orientation of each of the basic blocks.

When using origami blocks, most designs require nine blocks. However, some patterns need sixteen to see the overall effect of the pattern.

Block Setting—I

Let's look at some changes in design effected by varying the setting by one pattern block. Consider the example, Road to Oklahoma.

Juxtapose the blocks in one direction (5–6).
Change the direction of the blocks (5–7 and 5–8).
Change the colors of the blocks (5–9 to 5–12).

The image of the design changes when you lighten or darken a color or when you change the color of each block. Use your imagination, and color the blocks carefully, checking juxtaposed blocks.

Shoofly

Nine-Patch

Nine-Patch

↓ Nine-Patch

5–3 *Three* Nine-Patch *block combinations*

5–4 Shoofly *center-square print variations*

5–5 Shoofly *triangular print variations*

Road to Oklahoma
varied block settings

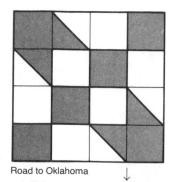

Road to Oklahoma

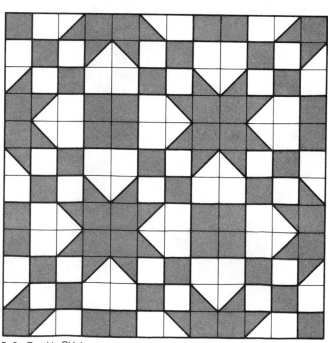

5–6   Road to Oklahoma *blocks facing same direction*

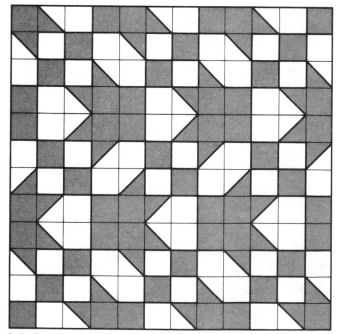

5–7   Road to Oklahoma *blocks facing different directions*

5–8   Road to Oklahoma *blocks facing different directions*

Road to Oklahoma
color changes (5–9 to 5–12)

5–9   Road to Oklahoma *color variation*

5–11   Road to Oklahoma *color variation*

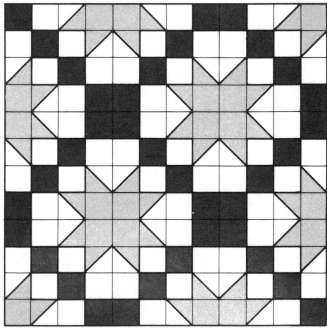

5–10   Road to Oklahoma *color variation*

5–12   Road to Oklahoma *color variation*

Adding Plain Blocks

5–13   Road to Oklahoma and Plain Block *design*

Placing Plain Blocks

If you mix the colors of the folded origami paper, the pattern unit becomes clear.

Now try as many settings as you can think of by getting ideas from the Four-Patch examples on these pages.

See 5–13 and 5–14 for how placement of plain blocks can influence quilt design. The basic block used is still Road to Oklahoma, combined here with plain blocks.

Color and Direction Variations

You can achieve multiple design possibilities from single blocks when the color and the direction of the block setting are varied. See examples 5–15 to 5–90 (pp. 123–128 and 145–157).

5–14   Road to Oklahoma and Plain Block *design*

Color and Direction Variations

Wild Goose Chase ↓

Split Nine-Patch ↓

5—15

5—17

5—16

5—18

123

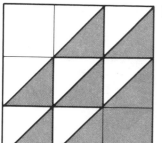

North Wind ↓

More Color and Direction Variations

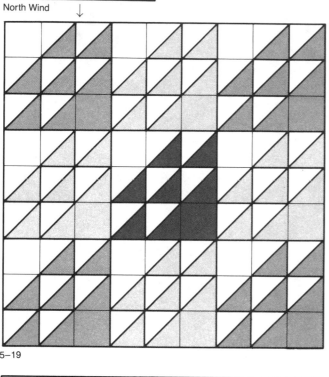

5–19

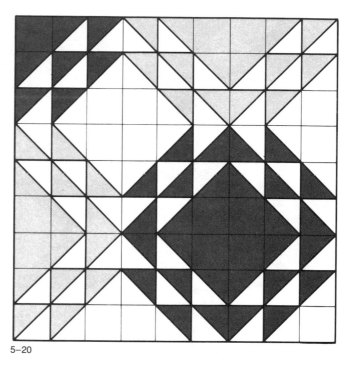

5–20

5–21

5–22

Monkey Wrench ↓

5–23

5–25 ↑

Mosaic

Pinwheel ↓

5–24

5–26

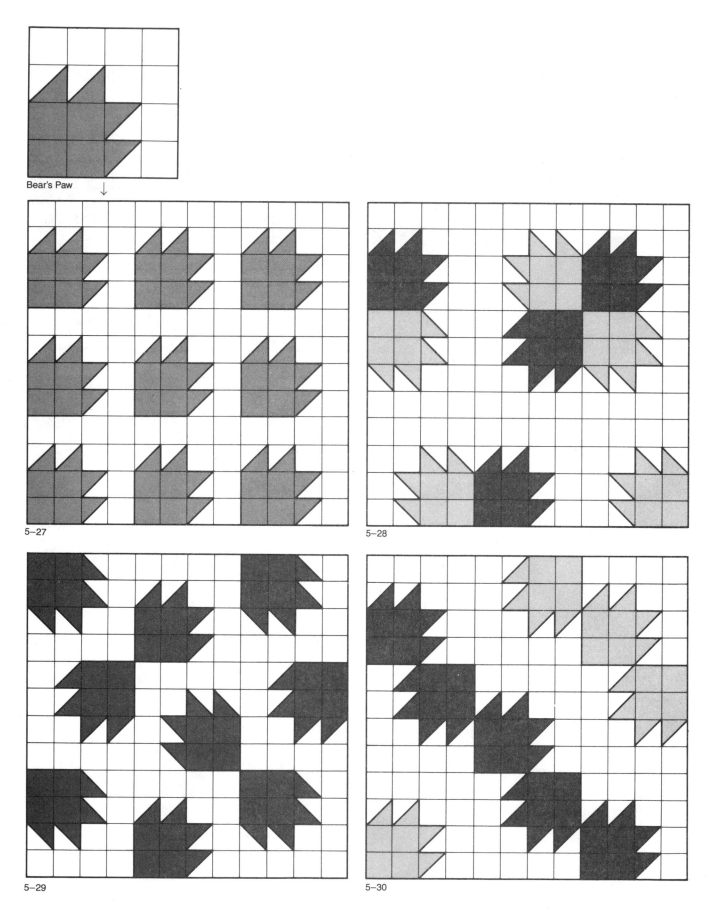

Bear's Paw

5-27

5-28

5-29

5-30

126

Ribbon Border Quilt ↓

5–31

5–32

5–33 ↑

Streak of Lightning

Swastika ↓

5–34

127

5–35

Lady of the Lake

Columns

5–36

Old Maid's Puzzle ↓

5–37

5–38

continued on p. 145

128

Original Designs by Japanese Quilters
using origami as a design tool

Made by Atsuko Yokoyama
100 × 87 inches (255 × 218 cm) cotton
See design on p. 8.

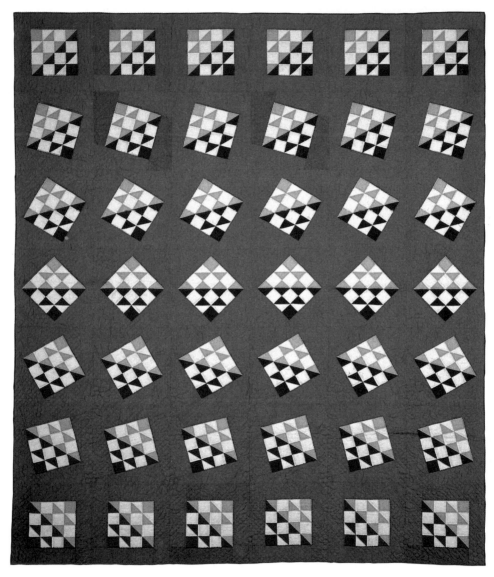

4–4 Made by Keiko Kitajima
93 × 80 inches (232 × 200 cm) cotton

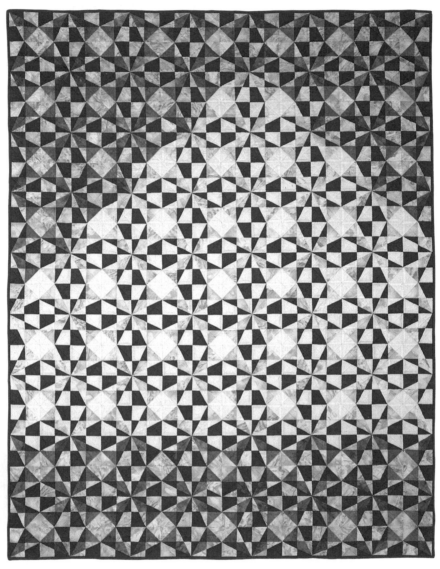

4–5 Made by Ritsuko Shino
83 × 65 inches (209 × 163 cm) cotton

4–6 Made by Mitsuko Iwata
99 × 79 inches (247 × 197 cm) cotton

4–7   Made by Mitsuko Makita
59 × 68 inches (149 × 170 cm) cotton

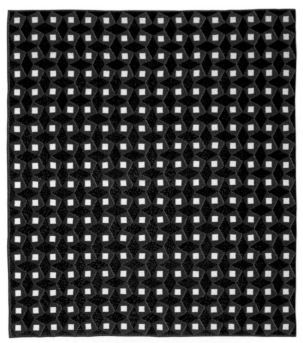

4–10   Made by Miyoko Shijo
90 × 80 inches (225 × 200 cm) cotton

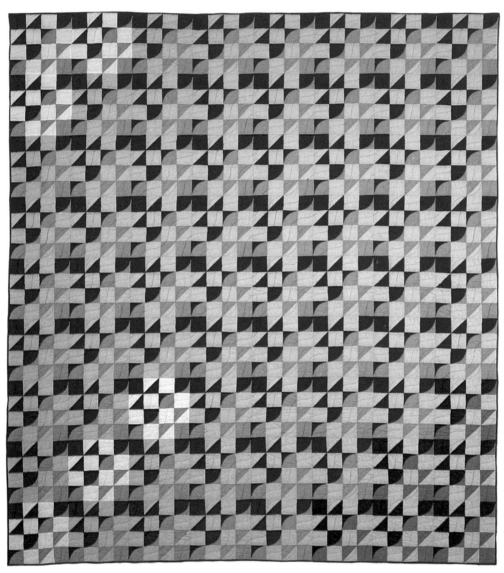

4–27 Made by Kiyoko Matsushima
87 × 77 inches (218 × 194 cm) cotton

4–28   Made by Kiyoko Matsushima
89 × 70 inches (224 × 176 cm) cotton

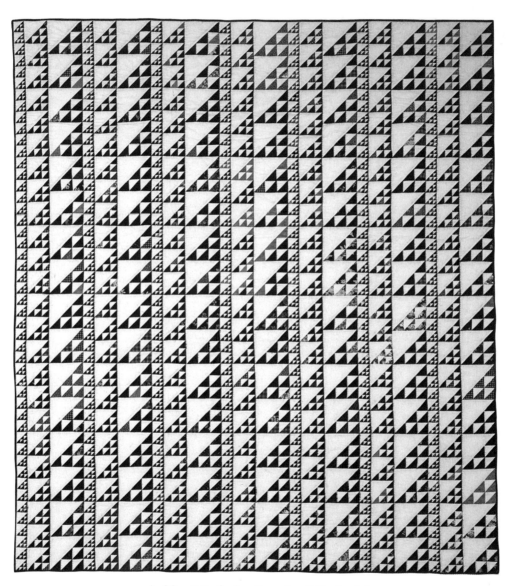

4–33 **Made by Junnko Miyazaki**
80 × 70 inches (202 × 177 cm) cotton

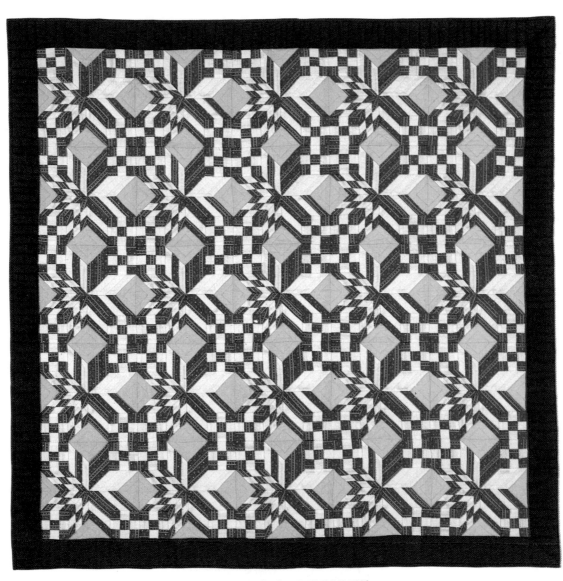

4–41 Made by Michi Miike
53 × 53 inches (134 × 134 cm) cotton

4–49 **Made by Kumiko Kimura**
100 × 80 inches (252 × 202 cm) cotton

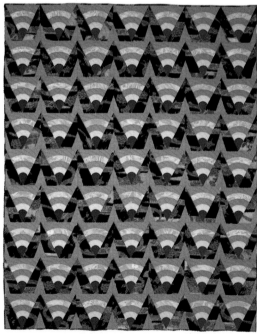

4–50 **Made by Harue Sato**
90 × 70 inches (227 × 177 cm) cotton

4–55 **Made by Ritsuko Shino**
82 × 72 inches (205 × 182 cm) cotton

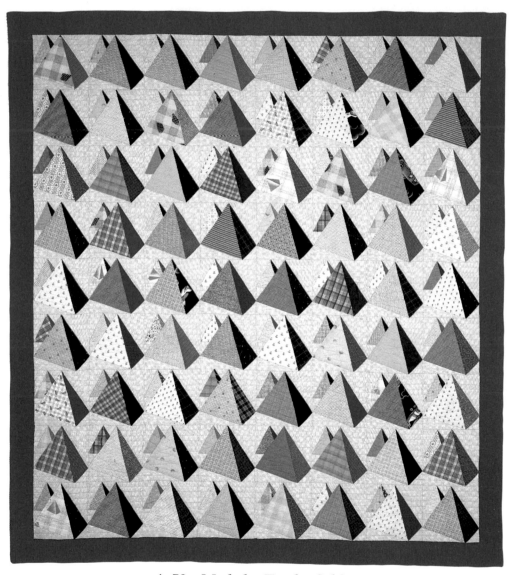

4–58 Made by Teruko Sekine
96 × 88 inches (240 × 220 cm) cotton

4–59 Made by Kiyoko Matsushima
29 × 29 inches (74 × 74 cm) cotton

4–61 Made by Harue Sato
87 × 68 inches (218 × 170 cm) cotton

4–63 **Made by Keiko Takahashi**
91 × 71 inches (229 × 179 cm) cotton

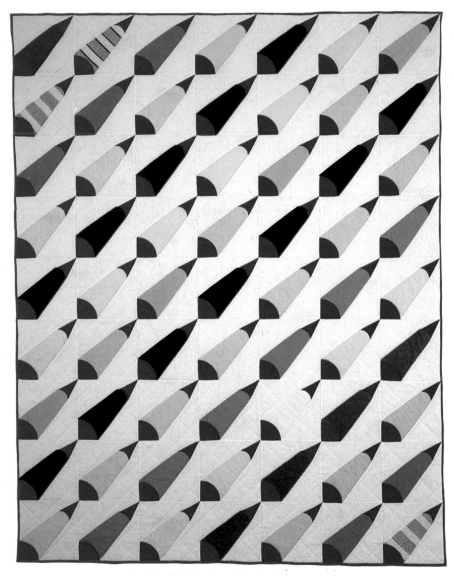

4–65   **Made by Machi Sasaki**
90 × 70 inches (227 × 177 cm) cotton

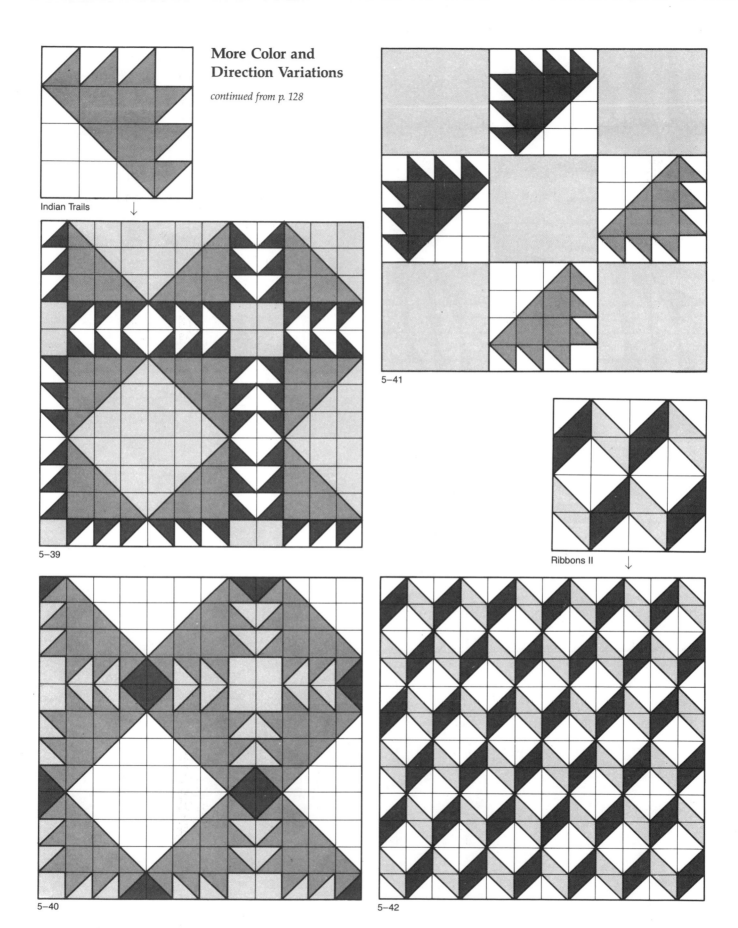

More Color and Direction Variations

continued from p. 128

Indian Trails

5—39

5—40

5—41

Ribbons II

5—42

Widows

5–45

July 4th

Cheyenne

5–44

5–46

146

5–47

5–48

Brave World

Six-Point Star

Key West Star

Rocky Road to Kansas

5–49

5–50

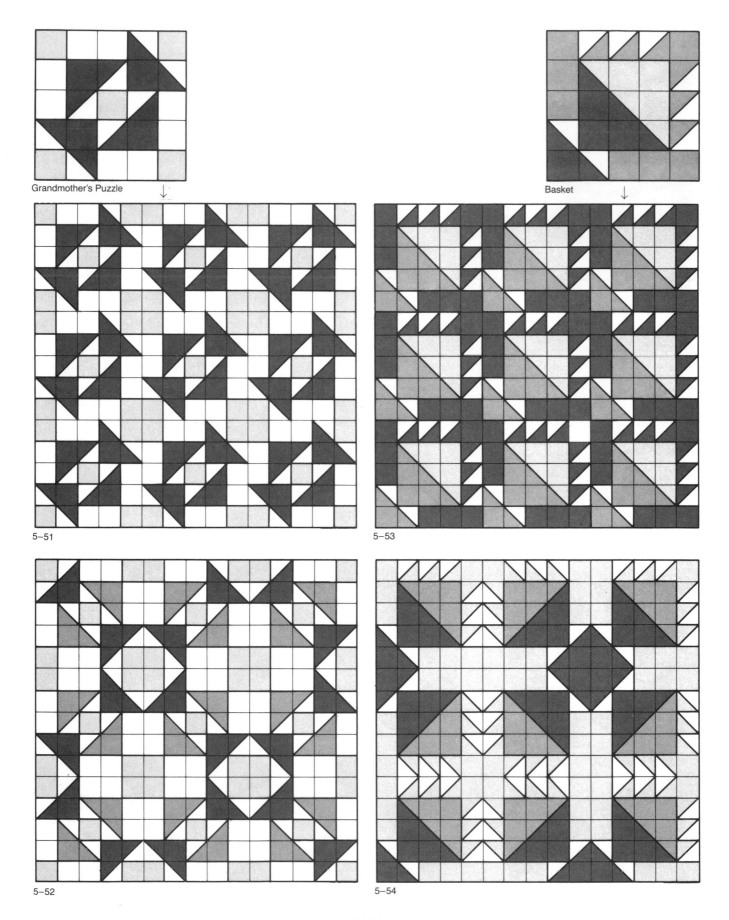

Grandmother's Puzzle

Basket

5-51

5-53

5-52

5-54

148

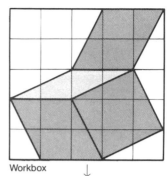

Workbox

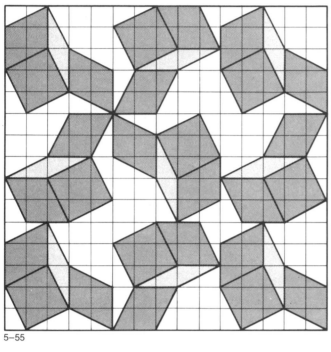

5—55

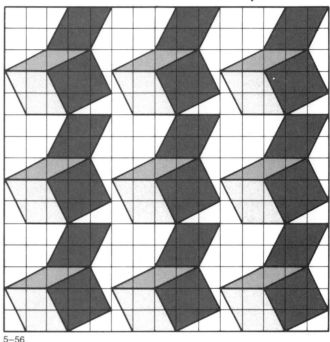

5—56

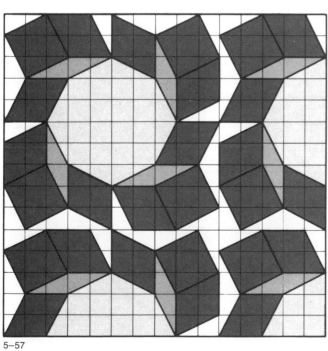

5—57

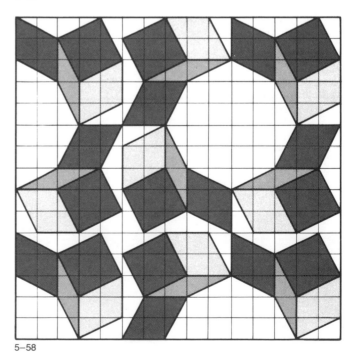

5—58

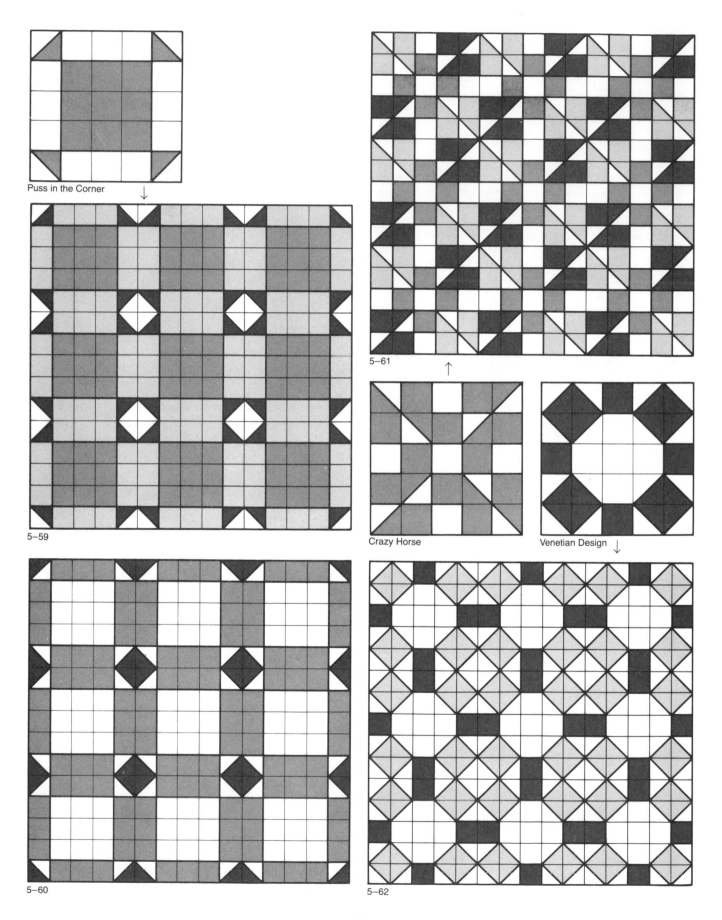

Puss in the Corner

5-59

5-61

Crazy Horse

Venetian Design

5-60

5-62

Basket

5-63

5-64

Flying Geese

5-65

5-66

151

5—67

Propeller

Rolling Star

5—68

Crown and Thorns

Ducks and Ducklings

5—69

5—70

5–71

5–72

Arrowhead Star

Rosebud

Chain

Wyoming Valley

5–73

5–74

153

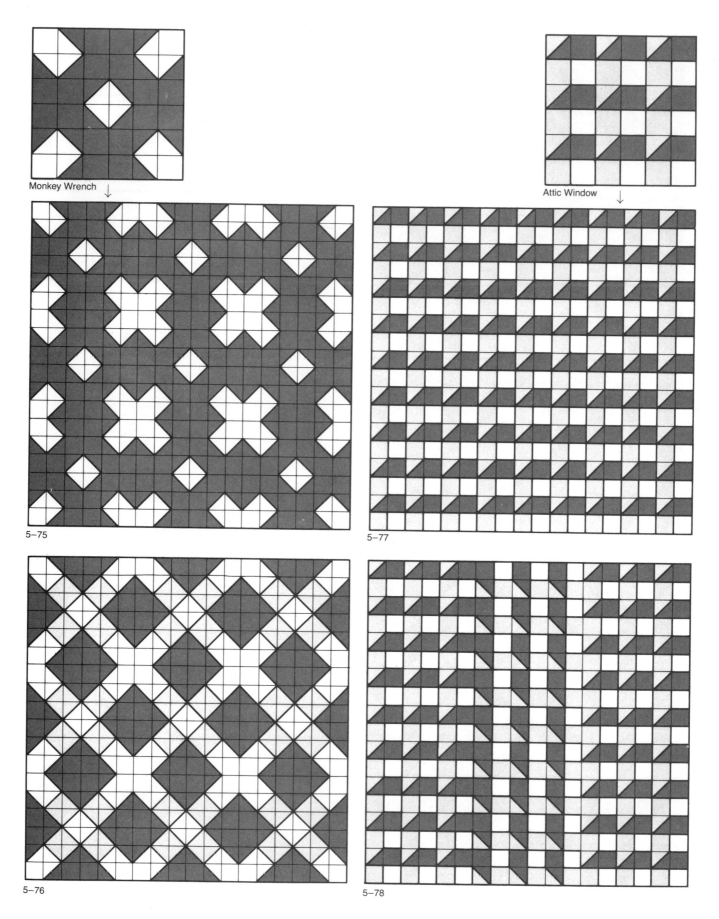

Monkey Wrench

Attic Window

5—75

5—77

5—76

5—78

154

Goblet

5—81

5—79

Flutter

Pine Tree

5—80

5—82

Unknown

5-83

5-85

Maple Leaf

5-84

5-86

Checkerboard ↓

5–87

5–88

5–89 ↑

Ozark Maple Leaves

Unknown ↓

5–90

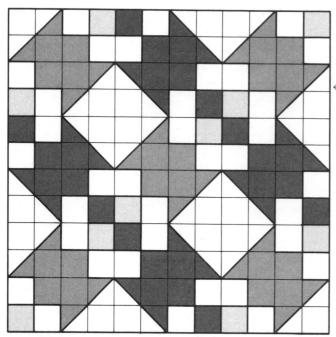

5-91 Ohio Beauty and Northern Star *design*

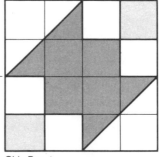

Ohio Beauty

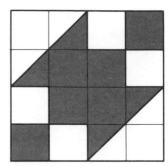

Northern Star

Block Setting II

Let's look at the changes made by combining two or three different blocks.

Using the four color changes, experiment with different settings to find new and effective combinations.

When you combine blocks of two or three different patterns, simply place the same grids together, and the lines will be continuous.

Don't throw away trial origami patterns. Try mixing them with new ones and you'll discover new possibilities.

You'll see on these pages combinations of two different blocks (5-91 to 5-101) and combinations of three different blocks (5-102 to 5-104).

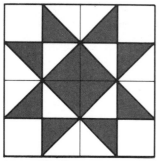

Kansas City Star

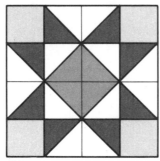

Unknown

5-92 Kansas City Star and Unknown *design*

5-93 Crazy Ann and Spools *design*

158

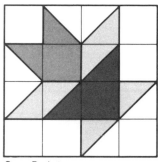

Scrap Basket

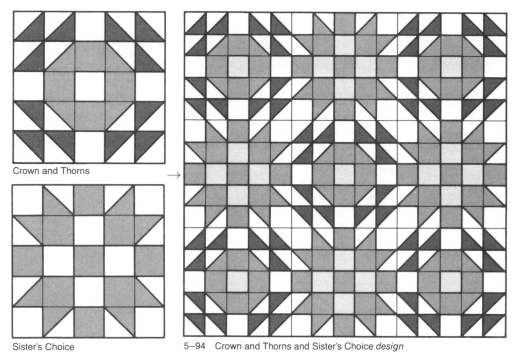

Crown and Thorns

Sister's Choice

5–94   Crown and Thorns and Sister's Choice *design*

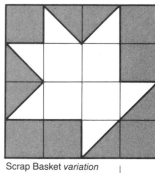

Scrap Basket *variation*

Two-Block Combinations
(5–93 to 5–101)

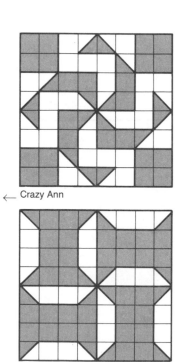

← Crazy Ann

Spools

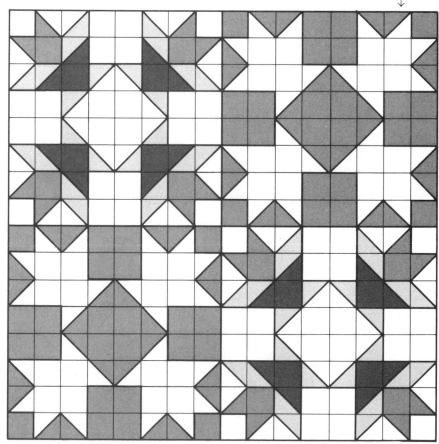

5–95   Scrap Basket and Scrap Basket *variation design*

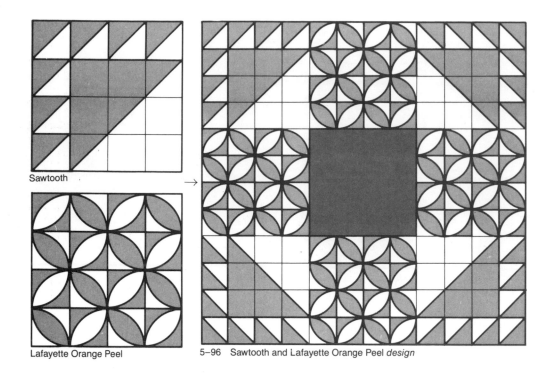

Sawtooth

Lafayette Orange Peel

5–96   Sawtooth and Lafayette Orange Peel *design*

5–97   Sawtooth and Lafayette Orange Peel *design*

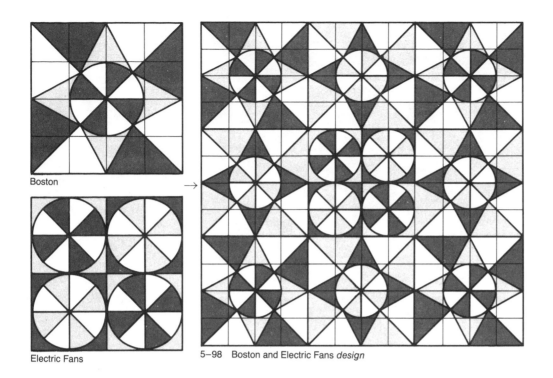

Boston

Electric Fans

5–98 Boston and Electric Fans *design*

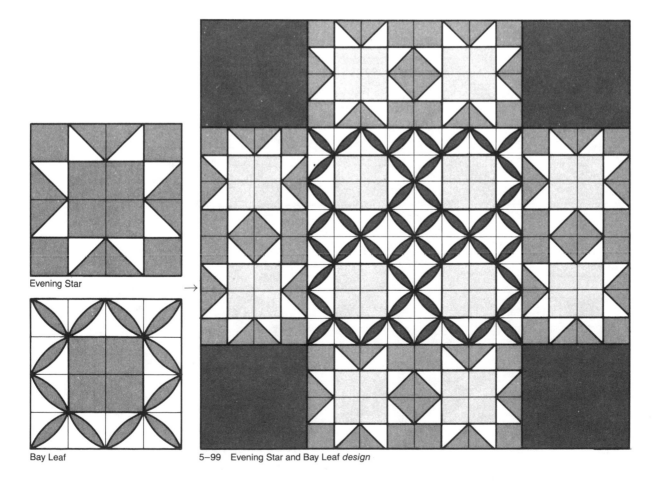

Evening Star

Bay Leaf

5–99 Evening Star and Bay Leaf *design*

161

Fifty-four Forty or Fight

St. Louis Star

5–100   Fifty-four Forty or Fight and St. Louis Star *design*

English Ivy

Steps to the Altar

5–101   English Ivy and Steps to the Altar *design*

Three-Block Combinations (5–102 to 5–104)

5–102 Anvil, Columns, and Electric Fans *design*

Anvil

Columns

Electric Fans

5–103 Anvil, Columns, and Electric Fans *design*

Eddystone Light

Nine-Patch

Capital T

T Blocks

5–105   Nine-Patch *design*

5–104   Eddystone Light, Capital T, and T Block *design*

5–105A   Strips

5–105B   Strip

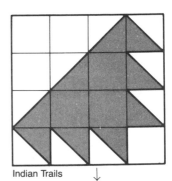

Indian Trails ↓

As you can see from the examples on these pages, different block settings can result in many different design possibilities.

First, it can simplify the actual pattern you make. When Nine-Patches are used with the same color in the four corners, you'll create a larger square (5–105). From this design you can see that you don't necessarily need to sew by the block. You can make this quilt quite easily by cutting and sewing long strips (5–105A and 5–105B), by keeping some margins or seam allowances for sewing and by cutting horizontally before combining.

The large squares in the Indian Trails pattern (5–106) or the large squares and rectangles at the bottom of the Baskets design (5–107) can be made without seam lines.

You can discover these ideas quickly through the setting process. This is one of the merits of using origami paper and techniques for block setting.

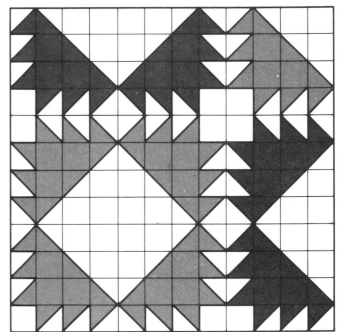

5–106 Indian Trails *design*

Basket → 5–107 Basket *design*

6

Making the Actual-Size Pattern

Making Your Own Templates

Many people think that copying ready-made sewing patterns is easier than making a new one. After all, books of patterns are published in abundance. However, if you depend on ready-made patterns, you won't be able to make your own original patterns, and the size and number of quilt designs you can make will be limited.

When you analyze designs with origami, making templates is not only easy, but it becomes simple to make any kind of pattern you want.

To complete a large work, like an album quilt or a big panel, you could ask others to share making part of it. If you organize a small community of quilters for your project, with each person contributing to the design, you'll immediately know the results.

In any case, making a quilt—even a small one—that's your own design, wrought from your own imagination, will be very satisfying.

Analyzing Pieces to Make Templates

A pieced quilt requires gathering small pieces of cloth to be sewn in easy, straight, and, sometimes, curved lines. If you have difficulty sewing, something must be wrong. Because of this relative simplicity many American and European women from earlier centuries made these quilts.

To join pieces involves mostly sewing in a straight line from edge to edge. You rarely sew up to a certain midpoint, then add another piece, or change directions.

Looking at some examples, let's try to find out how to determine the best and easiest way to sew straight lines. After the small section pieces have been joined, sew along the grids or the diagonal lines to complete a block.

The merit of practicing with origami is that it can be helpful for making actual-size patterns, too. Just use vellum or tracing paper in place of origami paper.

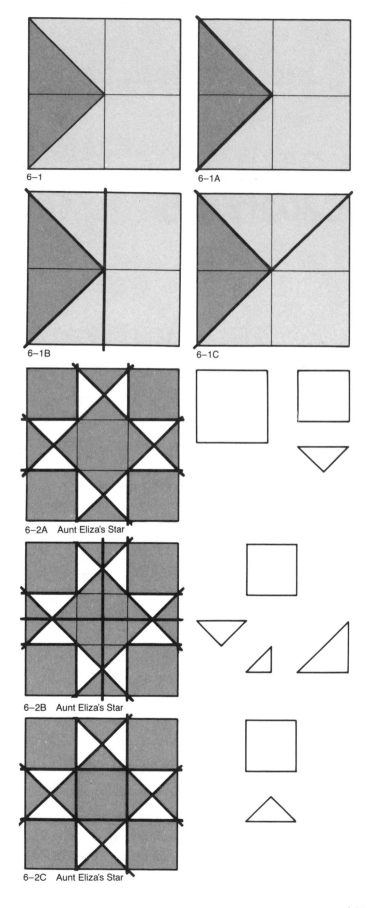

6-1

6-1A

6-1B

6-1C

6-2A Aunt Eliza's Star

6-2B Aunt Eliza's Star

6-2C Aunt Eliza's Star

The pattern shown in 6–1 can be analyzed as four grids. It is never patched in the way shown in 6–1A. The piecing in 6–1B and 6–1C are both appropriate ways, but the straight lines in 6–1C are better.

The thick lines in the illustrations indicate sewing lines. Depending on your analysis, the shapes of the actual templates change. It is up to you which pattern you use, but the use of shorter bias lines will produce better results.

Now let's find the lines in the traditional patterns. The pattern in 6–2A is without seam lines in the big central square. This is a repetition of one-fourth, and you can make it the way shown in 6–2B. Also, since it contains three grids, you can patch nine pieces. Depending on the pattern, there are many different methods you can successfully use to create your templates.

There are four ways to make the template for the block, Mrs. Morgan's Choice (6–9A to 6–9D), but it may become confusing if you patch together different shapes. The simplest way is to use triangles or rectangles shown in 6–9A.

Most of the five-grid and seven-grid patterns have central points; so, it should be easy to find lines to patch (6–10 and 6–11).

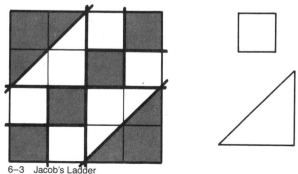

6-3 Jacob's Ladder

6–4A Rosebud

6–4B Rosebud

6–4C Rosebud

6–5A Goblet

6–5B Goblet

6–6A Waterwheel

6–6B Waterwheel

6–7A Ozark Maple Leaves

6–7B Ozark Maple Leaves

6–8 Six-Point Star

169

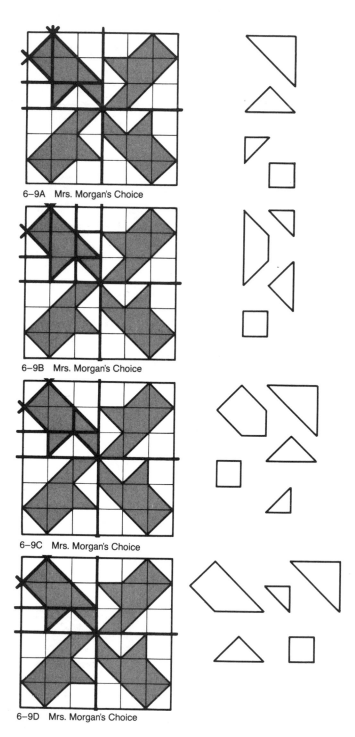

6–9A Mrs. Morgan's Choice

6–9B Mrs. Morgan's Choice

6–9C Mrs. Morgan's Choice

6–9D Mrs. Morgan's Choice

Making Actual-Size Origami Blocks

When the division lines have been decided, you make the actual-size pattern, without having to calculate to get the measurements for a given block. You just measure the length and the width with a string. By using string (instead of a ruler), the block can be subdivided easily. If it's a rectangle, divide the shorter side by the number of grids you want to have in the block. The length of one of your parts can serve as a template for your block.

Six Hints for Making Templates

The quality of paper you use must be close to that of the original small origami papers so that you can make creases easily and clearly. Make a square that matches the measurements you made with a string.

Fold Accurately

Fold the paper for block patterns just as you did the small origami paper since these papers will serve as patterns for cutting the cloth for your quilt.

Color the Template

If you color the same pattern in gradations of light and dark as in the design, mark them; then you can be more precise when cutting the cloth into two different patterns.

Cut Accurately

The necessary templates in the block must have clear lines, made with a ruler, so that you can cut accurately along the creases.

Paste Them on Cardboard

Choose a very firm paper—perhaps soft sand-paper or plastic—something that will prevent the edges of the patterns from becoming frayed after many uses. Paste the patterns on top of this base paper.

Mark the Margins

Add ¼-inch margins for seam allowances around the template. The importance of marking margins is that if you get used to marking the cloth for seamlines, you will always have to depend on these marks. That means you'll never improve your skills. The trick for improving is to cut the pattern with perfect ¼-inch margins and to train yourself to sew by sight. Even makers of mass-produced dresses do not mark each piece for a dress. Set the measurement for the margin and then cut accordingly.

Cut Fabric Accurately along the Markings

Use a good, sharp rotary cutter or scissors, and cut accurately along the marked lines. The templates must be numbered the same as the small origami pieces, and you should write the name of the pattern on each piece. Then everything will turn out perfectly.

When cutting many layers of fabric at one time, press them with a steam iron. The fabrics will stick together, making it easy to cut with accuracy.

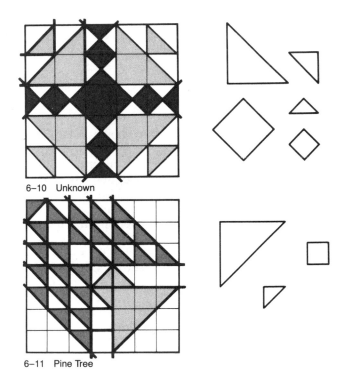

6–10 Unknown

6–11 Pine Tree

Index

About the Author

Born in Asahigawa, Japan, Kei Kobayashi has lived in New York since 1964. Originally a fashion designer, she designed women's apparel for her own company, KK Creations, from 1968 to 1986. Since the early 1980s, she has lectured and written numerous Japanese magazine and newspaper articles on American life, including food and the arts. She has written seven Japanese books, including the *Encyclopedia of American Patchwork Quilts* (1983), one of the first American quilt reference books in Japan. Ms. Kobayashi also wrote and produced a 30-minute television documentary, "American Quilters and Their Lives" (1988) for Japan's NHK-TV. In 1983, she brought a Shelburne Museum quilt exhibition to Japan and then produced an independent videotape, "The Quilt," based on the museum collection. She has curated many quilt exhibitions, notably Made in Japan: American Influence on Japanese Quilts, featuring Japanese quilters, for the New England Quilt Museum, the Parrish Art Museum, and the Japan Society of New York. She has also organized American culture tours for Japanese visitors to the United States.